chinese cooking

chinese cooking

BY

MARY WILSON

ILLUSTRATED BY DAVID REDMOND

OWLSWOOD PRODUCTIONS

Table of Contents

About the Author

With the publication of CHINESE COOKING, Mary Wilson realizes another goal in her culinary career. Having studied the cuisines of Europe, she now shares her knowledge and love of the cuisine she finds most exciting, Chinese cooking.

Years ago, while traveling Europe, Mrs. Wilson discovered her avocation: the art of fine cooking. She had always enjoyed the plain, hearty fare of her native Midwest but in Europe she discovered the sophistication of exquisite French sauces, remarkable Italian pastas and unforgettable Viennese desserts. Returning home from each trip she determined to master them all.

In 1960 when Mary and her husband moved to San Francisco, she embarked on the most challenging culinary adventure of all—Chinese cooking. Mary began her education at the source with trips to Chinatown, well-known restaurants, small tea houses and little-known Chinese cafes. She bought a wok and enrolled in cooking lessons. She studied with many of the Bay Area's finest teachers.

In 1970 Mary, herself, began teaching Chinese cooking, passing on to her students the knowledge she had gathered and offering it from a viewpoint western cooks really appreciate.

With unbounded enthusiasm, Mrs. Wilson fulfilled her ambition to study Chinese cooking in the Orient when she spent several weeks in Hong Kong and Taiwan on a true cook's tour. Cooking classes and visits to famed restaurants and their kitchens filled her days. In Hong Kong she studied at the famous Chopsticks Cooking Centre and in Taipei at the Pei Mai Institute.

In CHINESE COOKING, Mary Wilson offers a wide range of authentic recipes from the many regions of China plus her expert advice on equipment, techniques and ingredients.

Introduction

Suddenly Chinese woks, cleavers and chopping boards are familiar sights in kitchens across the country. The ancient art of Chinese food preparation has become today's discovery. Enthusiasm for this marvelous oriental cuisine is sweeping the western world for, I believe, abundant good reasons.

One of the most important reasons is its aesthetic appeal. From the preparation of the food, to its presentation and enjoyment, the Chinese have always insisted that each dish be a satisfying experience. It has to please every sense. The ingredients must be cut and combined in colorful array. The dish must have a pleasant aroma, interesting textures and, of course, delicious taste.

But there is even more appeal to Chinese cooking. Its emphasis on fresh, natural ingredients and cooking methods that retain nutritional content is a boon to anyone interested in good, healthful cooking.

And, people appreciate the economy of Chinese cooking. Vegetables are prime ingredients. Meats, fish and poultry are used in small but effective amounts. Dishes are cooked quickly and energy fuels are conserved.

Furthermore, in an era when so many people are trying to simplify their lifestyles, Chinese cuisine has been heartily welcomed. Except for the more elaborate banquet dishes, the foods are basically chopped, then stir-fried, steamed or braised. The seasonings and sauces are easily accomplished. And the necessary kitchen tools are few.

Though used through millennia, this way of cooking seems designed for today. Because a Chinese dish can be put on the table quickly, it is just the answer for working couples, hurried homemakers and everyone who must make minutes count in the kitchen.

But discover for yourself the many joys of Chinese cooking. I will teach you just as I do my classes, starting with equipment and techniques, adding notes on ingredients and accessories as we go along. The recipes are authentic. From the hundreds I have collected I have chosen those most appealing to the western palate. I suggest substitutes when possible and also give you a dependable mail order source for those ingredients not readily found in all areas.

So enjoy. Enjoy the chopping and slicing and arranging your preparation platter. Enjoy the stir-frying, the steaming, the red-cooking and all the cooking methods. And most of all, enjoy the deliciousness of the world's greatest cuisine, Chinese cooking.

The Great Wall
PEKING
Hwang Ho
Sian
Nanking
SHANGHAI
Wuhan
SZECHWAN
Yangtze • Chunking
FUKIEN
Si Kiang CANTON

Some Basic Equipment

Be assured you won't have to completely re-outfit your kitchen before you begin to cook the Chinese way. You can certainly make do with utensils you have on hand. A deep, heavy skillet can serve as a wok. A fine French knife can be used for cutting up the ingredients and you can stir-fry with two ordinary spatulas. However, as you proceed, you will see the advantages to using a few basic Chinese tools. You may purchase these utensils singly if you wish, or you may find them in handsome gift sets in many gourmet shops and department stores.

The Wok

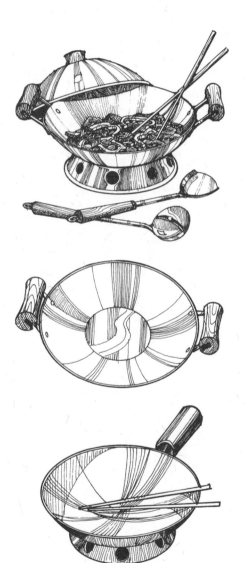

The most basic cooking tool in the Chinese kitchen is the wok. And once you start using one, it will become a basic in your kitchen, too. Used for centuries, the wok's functional round shallow design makes the most of a minimum of fuel. The sloped sides heat quickly and evenly. Foods can be stir-fried in just minutes. The wok can also be used for steaming, deep-frying, braising and smoking. If there is an all-purpose pan, the wok is it!

Because woks were designed to fit into open-top stoves, metal collars are needed to accomodate the wok to modern gas or electric ranges. These collars, called wok rings or fire rings, permit the wok to sit securely on the range just above actual contact with the heat source.

Originally made of cast iron, you will find woks now in spun steel, stainless steel, cast iron and aluminum. And there are many sizes and variations from which to choose. Woks range from 10 inches to 32 inches in diameter but a 12 or 14 inch wok is most suitable for family cooking. There are woks with metal handles, wooden handles, long "skillet" handles. There is even a flat-bottomed wok style which some people prefer to use with an electric range because it can be set directly on the burner without a wok ring. All are perfectly workable. Make your choice according to your own preference.

(What about electric woks? Because they cannot offer the high heat necessary for stir-frying, I can only recommend them for deep-frying, steaming and braising. An electric wok on the counter for those methods can indeed be handy.)

Remember, if you choose a cast iron or steel wok, it must be seasoned before it is used. To accomplish this, simply scrub the wok well with soap and water to remove any preservative oil. Dry it well. Next, rub cooking oil over the inside surface of the wok with a paper towel. Heat the wok until the oil begins to burn into the surface. Let the wok cool and wipe it with oil again. Reheat and continue the procedure several times until the wok begins to take on a deep brown color. This seasoning will prevent foods from sticking and will impart a very subtle flavor to the foods.

After cooking in your wok, it must be washed with mild suds (never scoured) and dried over heat. Before storing wipe the wok with a little cooking oil to prevent rust. With use, the seasoning will continue to build up until the wok is almost black inside. This is a sign of a well-used, well-loved wok.

The Spatula and Ladle

The art of stir-frying is most easily accomplished with a Chinese spatula and ladle. These are somewhat larger than their western counterparts and are designed to fit the curvature of the wok. The spatula is used to scoop up and toss foods rapidly in the wok. The ladle is used for removing foods from the wok and for ladling soup.

The Chinese Cleaver

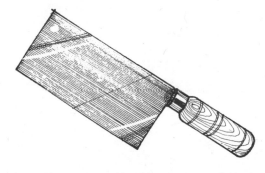

If the wok is the all-purpose pan, the Chinese cleaver is the all-purpose cutting tool. Although there are several kinds of Chinese cleavers, all have a straight back blade with a slightly curved cutting edge. The heavier cleavers are used for cutting bones, the lighter ones for chopping meats and vegetables. Besides chopping, the cleaver's broad blade is used to transfer minced and other hard to handle ingredients from the chopping board to the preparation platter. Care must be taken to wash the cleaver well and dry it thoroughly. (If the blade is carbon steel it is subject to rust.) To sharpen your cleaver, use a sharpening steel or hone it on the back of an earthenware plate.

The Chopping Board

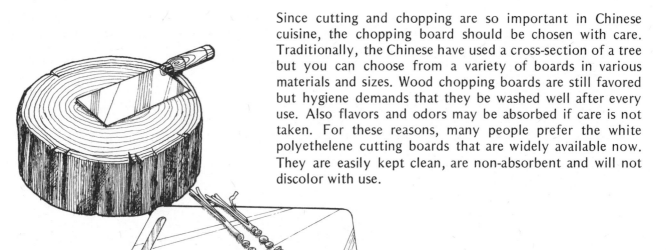

Since cutting and chopping are so important in Chinese cuisine, the chopping board should be chosen with care. Traditionally, the Chinese have used a cross-section of a tree but you can choose from a variety of boards in various materials and sizes. Wood chopping boards are still favored but hygiene demands that they be washed well after every use. Also flavors and odors may be absorbed if care is not taken. For these reasons, many people prefer the white polyethelene cutting boards that are widely available now. They are easily kept clean, are non-absorbent and will not discolor with use.

Kitchen Chopsticks

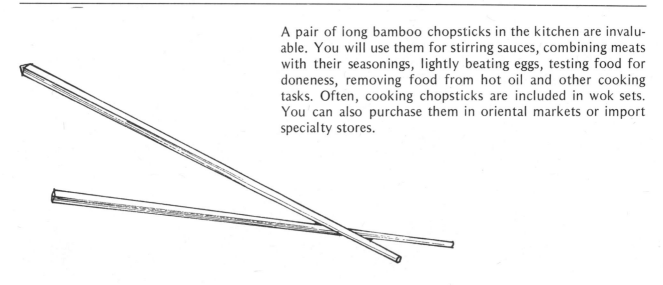

A pair of long bamboo chopsticks in the kitchen are invaluable. You will use them for stirring sauces, combining meats with their seasonings, lightly beating eggs, testing food for doneness, removing food from hot oil and other cooking tasks. Often, cooking chopsticks are included in wok sets. You can also purchase them in oriental markets or import specialty stores.

A Few Simple Techniques

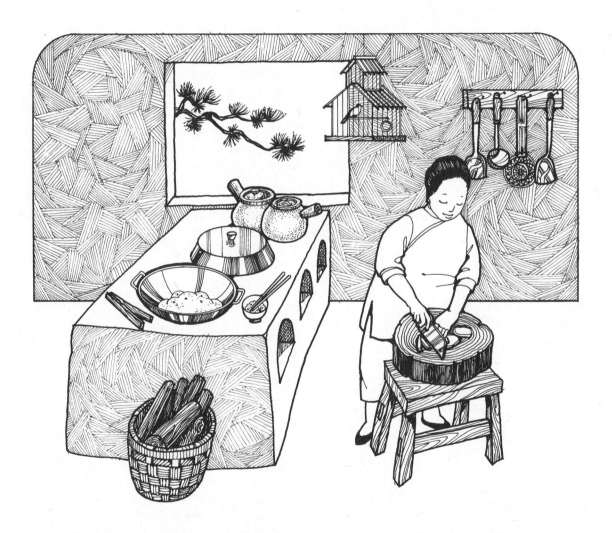

Because of the scarcity of fuel in China throughout the centuries, foods had to be cooked rapidly. Cooking methods had to be as efficient as possible and special techniques for preparing foods were developed. Once you become familiar with these techniques, you will, no doubt, incorporate them into all your cooking.

Preparing the Ingredients

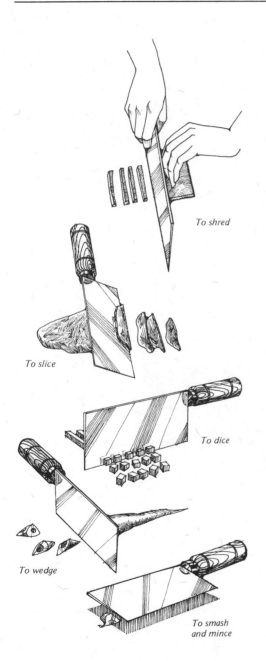

To shred

To slice

To dice

To wedge

To smash
and mince

It is true the Chinese spend more time preparing ingredients than actually cooking. This is because the preparation is of prime importance. The food is cut so it can be cooked quickly. You will note all the pieces in a dish are cut into a uniform size. This not only insures even cooking but also a pleasing appearance. These classic cuts include chopping, slicing, dicing, cubing, shredding, wedging and mincing. And you can accomplish them all with your Chinese cleaver.

To use the cleaver, pick it up and grasp it with your thumb and index finger just forward of the handle. Let the remaining fingers hold the handle comfortably. With your other hand hold the food with your fingertips tucked under. The knuckles should touch the side of the blade and serve as a guide while cutting. The cutting edge of the blade should be at a slight angle to the board. Lift the blade only about 1/4 inch above the food. The weight of the cleaver will do most of the cutting.

To slice: Cut slices 1-1/2 inches to 2 inches long, 1 inch wide and about 1/4 inch thick. When slicing meat, first cut into strips about 1-1/2 inches wide with the grain. Then slice across the grain diagonally. This exposes more meat surface for faster cooking and more tender results.
To shred: Cut matchstick-like strips about 1/8 inch by 1/8 inch by 1 to 1-1/2 inches long
To wedge: Cut into uniform triangular pieces
To cube: Cut into 3/4 to 1 inch cubes
To dice: Cut into 1/4 to 1/2 inch cubes
To chop: Cut into fine pieces about the size of a pea or smaller
To smash and mince: The cleaver is indispensable for preparing garlic and ginger. To prepare garlic, slightly smash the garlic with the broad side of the blade. Remove the outer covering, then smash the garlic, giving it a hard blow with the broad side of the blade again. Now the garlic can be finely minced with the sharp edge of the blade, scooped onto the blade and carried to the preparation platter. Do the same with peeled ginger slices, smashing them and then mincing them.

Blanching

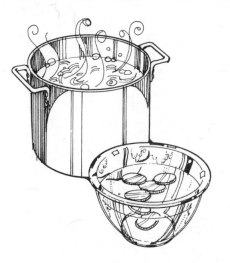

In order to save cooking time and to retain color and flavors, some vegetables must be blanched before they are stir-fried. To blanch, simply add the vegetable to a large pot of boiling water. Return the water to a boil and then turn off the heat. Let the vegetable remain in the water for the specified amount of time. Remove at once and immediately plunge into cold water to stop the cooking action. The blanched vegetable can be covered and refrigerated until it is ready to be used.

Cooking Methods

Many of the cooking methods used by the Chinese are much like those used by western cooks. However, there are subtle differences that make Chinese food unique in appearance and flavor.

Stir-frying is somewhat like the French sautéing. The wok is heated; oil is added and heated until it just begins to smoke. Then various foods are added, usually one kind at a time, cooked and removed. When every ingredient has been quickly cooked, the dish is combined and heated through. A sauce or glaze is added and the food is served at once.

The actual stir-frying technique consists of rapidly and continually scooping up the food with the spatula and turning it onto itself, in a tossing motion. This insures that all surfaces of the food are seared, the flavors are sealed in and the food is cooked in the least amount of time. A stir-fry dish can be completed in just minutes. The meat is always tender, the vegetables tender crisp.

Steaming is another important cooking method. It is fast and simple. The food is placed in a utensil equipped for steaming, covered with a lid and steamed. Meat, fish, vegetables and dumplings can be cooked this way.

You may want to include a steam plate, steam rack or bamboo steamer among your kitchen accessories. All of these can be used in conjunction with your wok.

Red-cooking is a slower process and is so-called because the food takes on a rich red-brown coloring. Often a large cut of meat or a whole chicken is prepared in this manner. Traditionally, the food is cooked over a low heat in a covered wok with soy sauce. As the sauce thickens it coats the food with a delicious glaze. If necessary, the food is then sliced or cut into bite-sized pieces and served.

Deep-frying is a favorite method because it not only seals in the juices and flavors but also provides a crisp coating to the food. Deep-frying is usually accomplished by cutting the food into cubes, coating it with a batter and carefully putting it into hot oil. The wok is an ideal utensil for deep-frying. Because of its shape, it only uses 2 or 3 cups of oil instead of the greater amounts called for in other deep-fryers. (Oil may be strained and reused several times. However, oil used to deep-fry fish should only be reused for fish.)

Shallow-frying uses a heavy skillet rather than a wok. The food is cooked in a scant amount of oil.

Accessories for Steaming

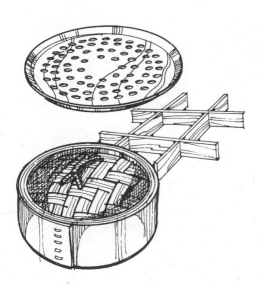

The steam plate is a round perforated metal plate that fits into the wok. You may place food to be steamed directly on the plate (to prevent sticking, lightly oil the plate first) or in a heatproof dish set on the steam plate.

The steam rack is usually made of two or four pieces of wood crossed so they rest against the sides of the wok, providing support for a dish. Food is placed in a heatproof dish and the dish set on the rack.

The oriental bamboo steamer can be used with the wok or with its own steamer pan. Meat and fish should be placed on a heatproof dish that can fit inside the steamer basket with the lid on. Vegetables and dumplings may be placed directly in the basket. Steamer baskets can be stacked, allowing several dishes to be steamed at once. Bamboo steamers are handsomely made and can be used as serving dishes.

Tools for Deep-Frying

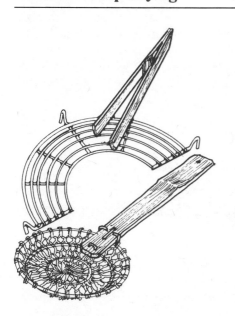

Bamboo tongs are an asset for all deep-frying. You'll find them ideal for placing food, one piece at a time, into hot oil, turning and separating pieces for efficient cooking, and for removing food quickly and easily. Made of wood, these tongs do not conduct heat and are always cool to handle.

The tempura rack, developed originally for Japanese tempura, works well for all types of food. The semicircular rack fits over the wok so that cooked food can be readily removed from oil. Placed on the rack, food stays warm while the oil drains neatly back into the wok. Food can then be placed on a serving platter.

The Chinese skimmer is a handsome utensil with a woven brass mesh strainer and long bamboo handle. This tool enables you to add or remove several pieces of food at once. The oil from the cooked food drains back into the wok and the food can be placed on paper towels before being removed to a serving platter.

Reading the Recipes

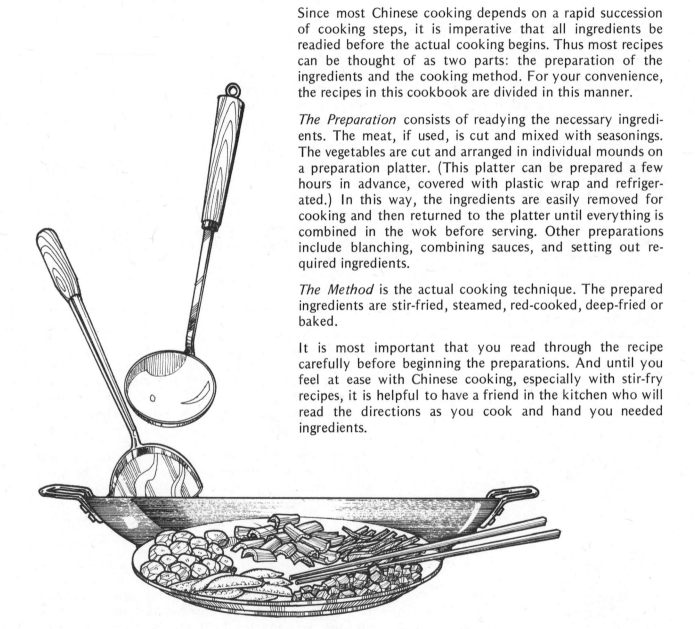

Since most Chinese cooking depends on a rapid succession of cooking steps, it is imperative that all ingredients be readied before the actual cooking begins. Thus most recipes can be thought of as two parts: the preparation of the ingredients and the cooking method. For your convenience, the recipes in this cookbook are divided in this manner.

The Preparation consists of readying the necessary ingredients. The meat, if used, is cut and mixed with seasonings. The vegetables are cut and arranged in individual mounds on a preparation platter. (This platter can be prepared a few hours in advance, covered with plastic wrap and refrigerated.) In this way, the ingredients are easily removed for cooking and then returned to the platter until everything is combined in the wok before serving. Other preparations include blanching, combining sauces, and setting out required ingredients.

The Method is the actual cooking technique. The prepared ingredients are stir-fried, steamed, red-cooked, deep-fried or baked.

It is most important that you read through the recipe carefully before beginning the preparations. And until you feel at ease with Chinese cooking, especially with stir-fry recipes, it is helpful to have a friend in the kitchen who will read the directions as you cook and hand you needed ingredients.

The Fun of Serving Chinese Food

One reason Chinese cooking has become so popular is that you can enjoy each dish as part of an everyday meal. Add extra broth to stir-fry dishes and they are marvelous one-dish dinners served over rice. Red-cooked meats are delicious with potatoes and a tossed salad. Steamed vegetables can become part of your mealtime, anytime.

However, when you become adept at several Chinese dishes, you will delight in serving a complete Chinese dinner. A typical menu includes a light soup, meat and fish entrées, steamed rice, dessert and tea. This menu can be translated to any number of guests. Remember, the Chinese do not double their recipes, they simply add another dish as the guest list increases. As a rule of thumb, you can use this ratio:

> Four people for dinner—a soup, two entrées, rice and dessert
> Six people for dinner—a soup, three entrées, rice and dessert
> Eight people for dinner—a soup, four entrées, rice and dessert

To make cooking the meal easier for yourself, serve only one stir-fry entrée. Round out your entrée selection with red-cooked dishes or steamed dishes that need no last minute attention. Make salads and desserts ahead of time.

The recipes in this cookbook indicate the number of people served. For example, a dish will serve 4 to 6 people, Chinese style, in conjunction with other entrée dishes at a Chinese dinner, but it will only serve 2 or 3 when it is served as the main entrée, American style.

Setting the Table

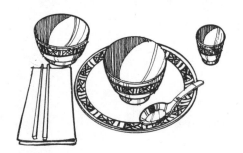

The Chinese, when eating at home, often use one bowl for both soup and rice and they often forego plates. Thus, chopsticks and a bowl comprise each place setting. At banquets, of course, the table setting is more elaborate. For your Chinese dinner you may wish to set each place with a soup bowl, a porcelain soup spoon, a rice bowl, a dinner plate, teacup and chopsticks. Serve the entrées colorfully garnished and mounded on platters or in serving dishes.

Serving Tea

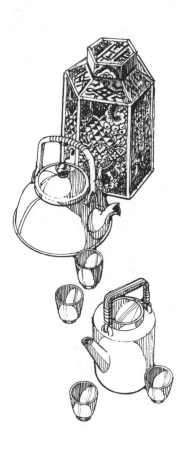

Tea is part of daily life in China. Every morning a large pot of strong tea is made in every Chinese household. Everyone, children included, drinks it. Tea is made to be sipped anytime of the day.

Teas are divided into black teas (called red teas in China) and green teas. The black teas are fermented, the green teas are not. There is also a semi-fermented tea called oolong. Black teas are robust and are preferred with seafoods. Green teas are refreshing and cool in flavor and are served with highly flavored and spicy foods. All teas can be embellished with blossoms to add delicious flavor and fragrance, for example, crysanthemum teas and gardenia teas.

To brew a pot of tea, the Chinese boil spring water in a brass kettle for just a few seconds. They then pour it over tea leaves in a warmed porcelain teapot. The tea is steeped and served. (Cream and sugar are never used.) When more tea is needed, boiling water is added to the teapot. Many people insist that the second pouring is more flavorful than the first.

You may serve tea to be sipped with your Chinese dinner or at its conclusion. Either way is perfectly acceptable. To make tea, boil a kettle of water for a few seconds. Rinse a teapot with a little of this water to warm it. Add tea leaves to the teapot and pour in the boiling water. Cover and let steep for 3 to 5 minutes. (Use 1 teaspoon of tea leaves per cup served.)

Of Course You Can Use Chopsticks

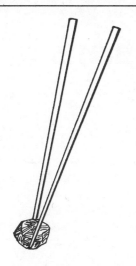

Chopsticks play an integral part in the Chinese meal. The foods, which are always bite-size, are meant to be savored individually. Chopsticks accomplish this. With chopsticks, you pick up one piece of food at a time, taking the time to enjoy its flavor and texture before going on to the next bite.

Here's how to use chopsticks. (a) Rest one chopstick in the hollow between your thumb and index finger and let the low part rest on the end of your ring finger. (b) Hold the other chopstick as you would a pencil so that the thumb, index and middle fingers hold it. (c) To pick up food, the index and middle fingers move the chopstick with the thumb serving as the pivot. Be sure the chopstick tips are even at all times. Tap them on your plate between bites if necessary. Be assured there is no one way to hold chopsticks. With practice, you will find a comfortable manner of your own.

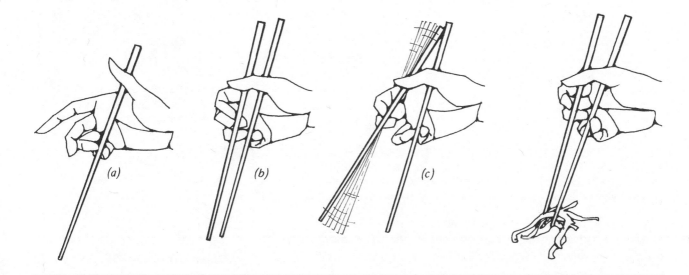

(a)　　(b)　　(c)

A List of Chinese Ingredients

Here is a list of those Chinese ingredients with which you may not be familiar. Each description provides information on what each one is, how it is used, where to find it, how to store it and, whenever possible, satisfactory substitutes. You can find many of these ingredients at your local supermarket; others you may have to search out in oriental markets. If, however, you do not live in an area where such shops are accessible, you can order many of these items by mail. For a mail order catalog, send $1.00 to The Chinese Grocer, 209 Post Street, San Francisco, California 94108.

Bamboo Shoots

Bamboo shoots add color and texture to Chinese dishes and absorb the flavors of the other ingredients.

Fresh bamboo shoots have a moister, sweeter taste than canned shoots but are often unobtainable since they are harvested only twice a year, in winter and spring. In season, you can find fresh bamboo shoots in oriental markets. They are about 4 inches in length and of a creamy, ivory color.

Canned bamboo shoots are more easily purchased since they are available in oriental markets and supermarkets across the United States. While there are many types, select the whole, unsalted bamboo shoots for the best flavor. To freshen canned shoots, rinse in cold water and let stand in water for 15 minutes before adding them to the recipe.

To store unused canned or sliced fresh bamboo shoots, cover with water and refrigerate in an airtight container for up to 3 weeks, changing the water several times a week.

You can approximate the crunchy texture of bamboo shoots by substituting carrots, sliced or cut into match-stick-size pieces. The carrots will add extra color, too.

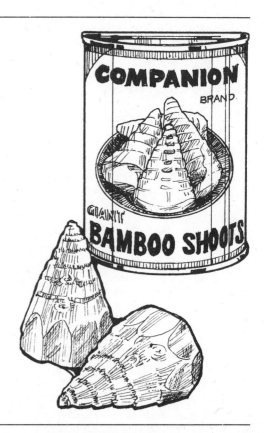

Bean Sprouts

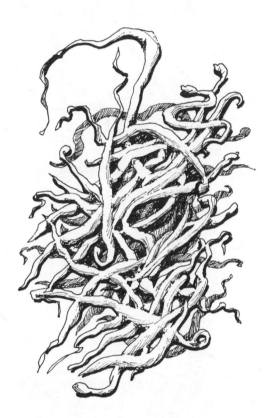

Because they are so easily grown, fresh bean sprouts can be found throughout the United States in many supermarkets, natural food stores and oriental markets. Usually, you will find them sold in bulk by the pound. They will have a white stem with a green or yellow nub at one end and a small root at the other. If the stems have a grayish or brownish color, they are not fresh and should not be purchased.

If possible, use fresh bean sprouts the same day you buy them. If you need to store them, rinse and drain them thoroughly, place in a plastic bag and refrigerate for up to 2 days.

To prepare fresh bean sprouts, rinse them thoroughly in cold water, removing any which are limp or beginning to discolor. Many Chinese chefs also remove the root and the nub from each sprout for a better appearance.

Canned bean sprouts are also available but they are not as flavorful as the fresh. If you have to use canned bean sprouts, drain them well and rinse several times in cold water. Keep unused canned sprouts covered in water in an airtight container in the refrigerator. If the water is changed daily, sprouts will last from 3 to 4 days.

Bean sprouts are excellent raw in salads, used as a garnish or cooked in any dish (although they are so delicate, only a minimal amount of cooking is ever required).

Shredded lettuce can be substituted for bean sprouts.

Cellophane Noodles

Cellophane noodles (also known as Chinese vermicelli and bean thread) received the name because of their white, transparent appearance. Made of bean starch, cellophane noodles are more delicate and less filling than wheat flour noodles.

Cellophane noodles come wound in a tight skein and are available in oriental markets. They are usually soaked before being cooked, but consult the recipe before doing so. These noodles require very little cooking, just enough to heat them through; care must be taken not to overcook them or they will become gummy.

Stored in a cool, dry place, cellophane noodles will keep indefinitely.

Rice sticks may be used in place of cellophane noodles.

Chili Paste or Sauce

This red-orange paste is made from minced red chile peppers, seasonings and other ingredients. Chili paste is *very* hot. Also called Szechwan paste, chili paste is often cooked in Szechwan recipes with fish, meats and vegetables in addition to its use as a table dip and relish. When using it for the first time, start with a very small amount, adding only half the amount indicated in the recipe, for example, and adding more to taste after sampling.

Chili paste is available in small cans in oriental markets. Some varieties come with soy beans or garlic; select the type you prefer.

Store unused chili paste in an airtight container in the refrigerator for up to 6 months.

As a substitute, use 4 to 5 drops Tabasco sauce for each 1/2 teaspoon chili paste.

Chinese Cabbages

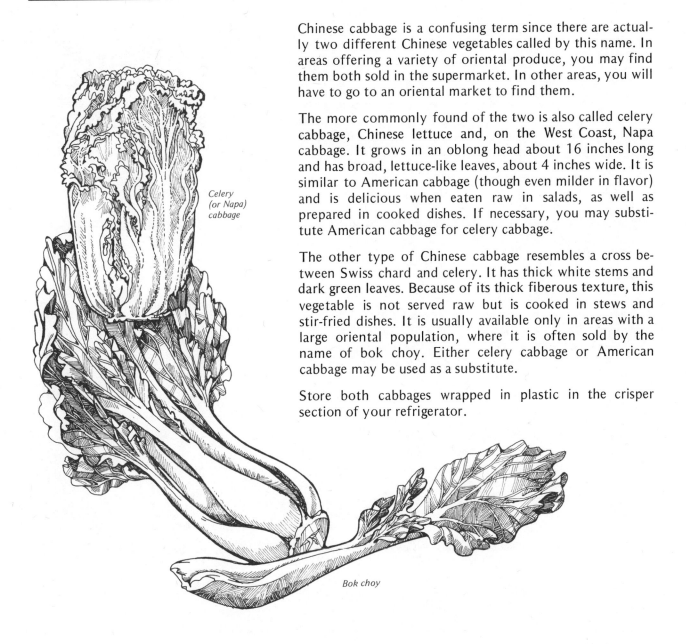

Celery (or Napa) cabbage

Bok choy

Chinese cabbage is a confusing term since there are actually two different Chinese vegetables called by this name. In areas offering a variety of oriental produce, you may find them both sold in the supermarket. In other areas, you will have to go to an oriental market to find them.

The more commonly found of the two is also called celery cabbage, Chinese lettuce and, on the West Coast, Napa cabbage. It grows in an oblong head about 16 inches long and has broad, lettuce-like leaves, about 4 inches wide. It is similar to American cabbage (though even milder in flavor) and is delicious when eaten raw in salads, as well as prepared in cooked dishes. If necessary, you may substitute American cabbage for celery cabbage.

The other type of Chinese cabbage resembles a cross between Swiss chard and celery. It has thick white stems and dark green leaves. Because of its thick fiberous texture, this vegetable is not served raw but is cooked in stews and stir-fried dishes. It is usually available only in areas with a large oriental population, where it is often sold by the name of bok choy. Either celery cabbage or American cabbage may be used as a substitute.

Store both cabbages wrapped in plastic in the crisper section of your refrigerator.

Chinese Parsley (Cilantro)

Chinese parsley, or cilantro, is an herb popular in many different types of cuisine. Although reminiscent of, and often used in the same manner as, American parsley, cilantro's flavor is very different.

Fresh cilantro may be available at your supermarket in the produce section or in specialty markets. To store, wash thoroughly, place stems in water and cover leaves with plastic wrap. It will last up to 1 week.

Dried cilantro may be used instead of the fresh variety and is available in the spice section of most supermarkets.

Chinese Wines

The term "wine" is used to refer to all Chinese alcoholic beverages, many of which are not wine-like at all. Since grapes are not available in China, these wines are made from various other ingredients, including rice (with and without spices), other grains and fruits. Chinese wine can be either distilled or fermented and the alcoholic content can vary greatly from wine to wine.

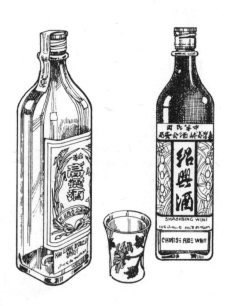

In cooking, the two wines most called for are Shoa Hsing (also known as yellow wine) and Kaoliang. While both are difficult to obtain in America, each has a satisfactory substitute. Shoa Hsing, a rice wine, has a flavor similar to dry cocktail sherry. Kaoliang, a very potent, flavorless liquor distilled from grains, can be replaced by vodka or gin in recipes.

As a beverage, Chinese wines are traditionally consumed only at meal times and may be served warmed, like Japanese saké. There are, however, no strict rules concerning beverages, so feel free to serve whatever you prefer.

Cloud Ear Fungus Mushrooms

Like black mushrooms, cloud ears are a member of the fungus family. Sold in oriental markets, cloud ears are dried, about 1 inch long and a blackish-brown color. If possible, buy the smaller size cloud ears; although more expensive, they are more delicate and tender than the larger.

Before using, rinse cloud ears, place them in a bowl and cover with very warm or hot water, using about 1/2 cup for every 4 cloud ears. During soaking, they will expand to several times their original size and take on a mushroom-like flavor and texture. Soak 15 to 20 minutes, or until tender. Remove the small hard core from each and prepare as indicated in the recipe.

Dried cloud ears will keep indefinitely in a cool, dry place if stored in an airtight container.

Although more flavorful than cloud ears, dried black mushrooms may be substituted for cloud ears in soups and other dishes.

Daikon Radish

Although the daikon radish resembles a large, white carrot, its flavor is reminiscent of the turnip. Each radish is from 6 to 15 inches in length, from 2 to 4 inches in diameter and has a crisp, white flesh and piquant taste. Look for it in the produce section of oriental markets and in some supermarkets.

Daikon radish is enjoyed raw in salads or cooked in soups and stir-fried dishes. When preparing daikon, break off the required amount and peel off the outer skin. Store the remaining portion unpeeled and unwrapped in the crisper section of your refrigerator. It will last up to two weeks.

If you are unable to find a daikon radish, substitute a white icicle radish or a very fresh turnip. Soak grated or sliced turnip in ice water for 15 to 20 minutes before using since its flavor is stronger than that of the daikon.

Dried Black Mushrooms

The distinctive flavor of black mushrooms complements a great number of Chinese dishes from soups to all manner of entrée dishes. While their flavor is stronger and quite different from western mushrooms, you may use canned or fresh western mushrooms as a substitute.

Black mushrooms are sold dried in small packages or boxes in oriental markets. Generally there are three types available which may be used interchangeably. The Hana mushroom is thicker and recognizable by the cracks in its surface. It has the better flavor and is accordingly more expensive. The Jyo and Nami mushrooms are somewhat thinner, less flavorful and not as costly.

To prepare dried black mushrooms, rinse and place them in a bowl; pour very warm or hot water over them, using about 1/2 cup water for every 4 mushrooms. Allow to soak for 15 to 20 minutes, or until tender. Squeeze excess liquid from the caps and cut off the tough parts from the stems. Use as directed in recipe. Reserve the liquid in which mushrooms have been soaked and use in place of water or broth in soups, stir-fry and sauce dishes.

Dried mushrooms keep indefinitely if stored in a cool, dry place in an airtight container.

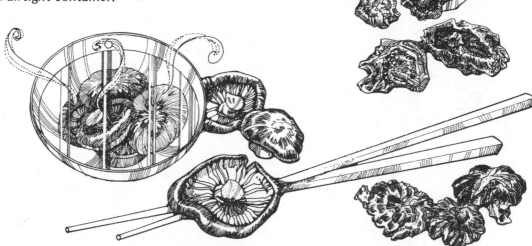

Fermented Black Beans

Fermented black beans are popularly used as a condiment after being fermented and salted. In this form, they are available in plastic bags or cans in oriental markets. Before using fermented black beans in any dish or sauce, they must be washed to remove the salt; if they are not, the flavor will be too strong. Soak the required amount of beans in water for 15 minutes and then rub gently, but thoroughly, to remove the salt. Rinse again.

To make black bean sauce, mash washed fermented beans with a mortar and pestle, or a fork, and combine with smashed garlic. Use 1 clove garlic for each tablespoon of black beans. Stir-fry this mixture in wok for 1 to 2 minutes, or until you detect the aroma of the garlic. Sauce is now ready to be used in stir-fried or steamed dishes, as indicated in the recipe.

Fermented black beans will last up to 1 year in an airtight glass jar in the refrigerator. Add a small amount of cooking oil (preferably peanut oil) if beans seem to be drying out.

There is no substitute for fermented black beans.

Five Spice Powder

Five spice powder is, as its name indicates, a special blend of spices. Recipes may vary, but you will usually find it to be a combination of ground star anise, cinnamon, cloves, ginger and fennel seed. Look for it in the spice section of your local supermarket or in oriental markets, in bulk and packets. In cooking, five spice powder masks unwanted odors in addition to adding a unique, spicy flavor.

If you are unable to obtain ready-made five spice powder, you can whip up this recipe at home:

1 teaspoon fennel seed   1 teaspoon ground cinnamon
1 teaspoon aniseed   1/2 teaspoon ground ginger
1 teaspoon ground cloves

Put fennel seed in blender and process until seeds are half

pulverized. Add aniseed and pulverize mixture completely. Add ground cloves, cinnamon and ginger. Process until all are well blended. This recipe may be doubled.

Store both commercial and homemade powder in an airtight container in a cool, dry place for up to one year.

Ginger Root

Ginger root is a versatile and indispensable item in any Chinese kitchen. As a condiment, it is valued for its sharp, piquant taste and is sliced, minced, grated or smashed, depending on the method of preparation and flavor desired. Ginger also acts as a flavor absorbing agent during cooking; just a 1/4 inch slice will remove unwanted odors and tastes from any dish, particularly seafood. Medicinally, tea made from ginger root is refreshing and soothing.

Ginger root is available by the pound in some supermarkets and in Chinese markets. Gnarled and golden brown in color, the irregular, almost flat pieces usually measure about 4 inches in length and an inch or two in diameter.

To store whole fresh ginger, scrub it gently with a vegetable brush, dry thoroughly and keep it in a brown paper bag in the refrigerator, where it will last up to 1 month. For longer storage, wash, dry and cut ginger into 1/4 inch slices. If kept in a plastic bag in the freezer, these ginger slices will last up to 6 months. Or, put slices into a screwtop jar, cover with dry sherry or rice wine, seal tightly and store in a cool place; this mixture will keep indefinitely.

Powdered ginger is not a substitute for ginger root.

Golden Needles

Golden needles, a part of the tiger lily flower, are used in Chinese cooking as a special garnish. Their distinctive, slightly pungent, musty taste goes well with soups, meats and poultry dishes.

In oriental markets, you'll find them as dried yellow-brown colored sticks or stems, about 2 to 3 inches long. If possible, select those of the palest gold color, as they are the best quality.

After being soaked in warm water for 15 to 20 minutes, golden needles double in size and become soft and pliable. Many people prefer to discard the tougher bulb end before adding them to recipes. In Mandarin cuisine, each golden needle is tied in a knot in the middle for elegance.

Dried golden needles will keep indefinitely if well wrapped and stored in a cool, dry place.

There is no substitute for golden needles.

Hoisin Sauce

Hoisin sauce, a thick, reddish brown sauce with a sweet, spicy taste, is widely used in Chinese cooking as an ingredient in sauces, marinades and dips.

Although ingredients may vary according to the manufacturer, the type of hoisin sauce you are most apt to find in cans in oriental markets is made of soy beans, wheat flour, sugar, water and various spices and seasonings. Hoisin sauce may also be made from a variety of vegetables and fruits, such as pumpkins, tomatoes, peppers and plums.

To store unused sauce, transfer it to a glass jar. Tightly sealed and refrigerated, hoisin sauce will last one year.

There is no substitute for hoisin sauce.

Loquats and Litchis

Two delicious fruits you'll enjoy in a variety of Chinese dishes are loquats and litchis (or lychees). Loquats are about 2 inches in diameter and orange in color. Their flavor is reminiscent of peaches and apricots, which may be substituted for canned or fresh loquats. Litchis are smaller, about 1 inch in diameter, oval in shape with a large center pit. Their white, fleshy pulp is covered by a rough, red skin. Canned white grapes or chopped pears may be substituted for fresh or canned litchis. Both loquats and litchis are favorite ingredients in dessert dishes; litchis are also popularly found in chicken, duck and sweet pork dishes.

While you may be lucky enough to find fresh litchis at oriental markets during June or July, fresh loquats are very difficult to obtain in America. Fortunately, both fruits are also sold dried in small packages and in cans with syrup.

Once opened, you can store canned fruit in its syrup in an airtight container in the refrigerator for up to one week. Dried or unopened canned fruit will keep indefinitely in a cool, dry place. Fresh fruit may be wrapped in plastic and stored in the refrigerator for up to one week.

Oyster Sauce

While oyster sauce actually is made from oyster extracts and soy sauce, this thick brown sauce has no fishy or oyster taste. Rather, it has a smooth, salty flavor which enhances the natural flavors of foods prepared with it.

Oyster sauce is sold in bottles and cans in oriental markets. There are different grades. The most expensive has a purer flavor and is used for dipping sauces. The less expensive grades are saltier and more pungent but fine for stir-fry dishes. If tightly sealed and stored in the refrigerator, oyster sauce will last indefinitely.

There is no substitute for oyster sauce.

Plum Sauce

Chinese plum sauce is a thick, piquant, fruity flavored sauce, similar to chutney. The most commonly used plum sauce is reddish brown and made from plums, apricots, chiles, vinegar and sugar. It is primarily used as a table condiment but is cooked in some dishes. If you like its spicy flavor, try it in place of sweet and sour sauce.

Chinese plum sauce is available in jars and cans in oriental markets. To store unused sauce, keep it refrigerated in a tightly sealed jar for up to 6 months.

If you are unable to purchase Chinese plum sauce, you may use this recipe:

1 (14 oz.) can purple plums, drained and liquid reserved
1 (8 to 10 oz.) jar apricot preserves
1/3 cup rice wine vinegar or white distilled vinegar
2 tablespoons sugar
2 dried red chiles, crushed *or* 5 to 6 dashes Tabasco sauce
1 clove garlic, smashed and minced
1 tablespoon smashed and minced ginger root
1/2 to 3/4 cup liquid reserved from canned plums

Remove plum pits and quarter plums. In a bowl, combine plums, apricot preserves, vinegar, sugar, chiles, garlic and ginger. Add enough reserved plum liquid to easily combine ingredients. (For a smoother texture, you can liquify sauce in a blender for a few seconds.) In a saucepan, bring sauce to a boil over high heat, stirring occasionally. Lower heat to simmer and cook for 20 minutes, until sauce thickens. Stored in a tightly sealed glass jar, plum sauce will last 3 to 4 months. (Makes about 2 cups.)

Rice Sticks

These spaghetti-like noodles are made of rice flour rather than wheat flour. You can find them in oriental markets. Since they are dried, rice sticks will keep indefinitely if well wrapped and stored in a cool, dry place.

Rice sticks can be prepared in several different ways, so consult the recipe for cooking instructions. One method is to soak rice sticks in water for 20 to 30 minutes before adding them to a soup or stir-fry dish. Another popular way is to deep-fry rice sticks; while frying, rice sticks will expand up to 5 or 6 times their original size, so fry only a small handful at a time.

If necessary, you may substitute cellophane noodles.

Rice Wine Vinegar

Rice wine vinegar is a very mild, clear vinegar frequently used in Cantonese sweet and sour dishes. Its delicate flavor is also excellent in salad dressings.

Rice wine vinegar is available in bottles in oriental markets. Tightly sealed in a cool, dry place it will last indefinitely.

As a substitute for rice wine vinegar, white distilled vinegar may be used.

Sesame Oil

Oriental sesame oil is an amber colored, carefully prepared oil made from toasted sesame seeds. It *must not* be confused with the blander, less expensive sesame oil often sold in natural food stores.

In Chinese cooking, sesame oil is valued as a flavoring and aromatic agent rather than as a cooking oil. When used with foods being cooked, it should be added only in the last few minutes, since excessive heat destroys its flavor. Use it sparingly; its nut-like flavor is so pervasive just a few drops are sufficient in most dishes.

Purchase sesame oil in bottles in oriental markets. If kept in a cool place, sesame oil will keep indefinitely.

There is no substitute for oriental sesame oil.

Snow Peas (Chinese Peapods)

Snow peas or Chinese peapods are popular all over the United States because of their wonderfully sweet, crisp flavor. For this reason, you may find fresh snow peas in local supermarkets or oriental markets. Select the smaller, more tender pods and use as soon as possible after purchase. If necessary, you can store peapods in a plastic bag in the crisper section of your refrigerator for up to one week. Before using fresh snow peas, remove the stems and strings from them as you would from a string bean. Wash and let them stand in ice water for about 15 minutes before you intend to use them.

Snow peas are usually available in the frozen food section of your local supermarket. When using frozen snow peas (or other frozen vegetables in Chinese recipes), partially defrost to separate before using.

Whether fresh or frozen, snow peas are so tender that they require very little cooking (which makes them a popular ingredient in stir-fried dishes).

You may substitute green peas or peeled, sliced broccoli stems for snow peas.

Soy Sauce

Authentic soy sauce is a liquid brewed from fermented soy beans, parched wheat, salt and water. In Chinese cuisine, there are two distinct types of soy sauce, light and dark. Both are used to heighten the natural flavors of foods.

Dark soy sauce is thicker, sweeter and is used as much for the rich color it gives food as for its flavor. Light soy sauce is saltier, and used to delicately color lighter foods, such as pork or chicken, as well as being used as a table sauce.

While the imported Chinese soy sauce is preferable for Chinese dishes, it is usually only available in Chinese markets. If necessary, you can successfully substitute Japanese soy sauce; "Kikkoman" brand sauce is now manufactured in America and is available throughout the country in most supermarkets.

Kept in a cool, dark place in a tightly closed container, soy sauce will last indefinitely.

Light (or thin) soy sauce

Dark (or black) soy sauce

Star Anise

A favorite spice unique to oriental cooking is star anise. Its name is particularly descriptive since its flavor resembles western anise and each whole clove is an 8-pointed star. It is very aromatic and most often used in red-cooked dishes.

Star anise is sold whole in oriental markets in small packets. Whole pieces are about 1/2 to 1 inch across and brown in color. Because they are so brittle, stars are often broken. If necessary, tie 8 star points in a piece of cheesecloth and use in place of a whole star. Remove star anise before serving.

Stored in a cool, dry place in an airtight container, star anise will last up to 1 year.

A few drops of anise extract may be used in place of star anise.

Szechwan Peppercorns

These reddish brown peppercorns are similar to western black peppercorns but have a much hotter flavor and more aromatic scent when heated or crushed. (If necessary, however, cracked black peppercorns may be substituted in most recipes.) Szechwan peppercorns are available in oriental markets either loose or in small packets.

To get the true Szechwan pepper flavor in recipes, heat a small quantity of peppercorns in a skillet until they begin to turn dark brown. Be careful, they burn quickly! Allow peppercorns to cool and crush with a rolling pin or mortar and pestle; use according to the recipe.

Ground Szechwan pepper is frequently used combined with salt (equal parts of each are heated together for a short time) for a dry table dip.

In a tightly sealed jar, Szechwan peppercorns will keep indefinitely in a cool, dry place.

Tofu (Bean Curd)

Tofu, a custard-like food made from soy beans and water has been an important, inexpensive source of protein in oriental cuisine for centuries. Almost tasteless itself, tofu is easily, deliciously incorporated into all types of recipes, taking on the flavors of the foods and seasonings with which it is prepared. Because of its exceptional food value, tofu is becoming popular in the United States and can be found both fresh and in cans in many supermarkets and natural food stores as well as in oriental markets.

Fresh tofu is normally sold in 3 by 3 by 1 inch cakes, packed in water. Package sizes vary depending on the type of tofu, but average about 1 pound. Select the Chinese style which is firmer and more easily stir-fried than the Japanese style.

Before using, wash and drain tofu, and place between two plates or two pieces of paper towel, sandwich-style. Place a glass or similar object on top and allow tofu to stand for about 30 minutes. This helps to remove excess moisture from the cake.

To store fresh tofu or leftover canned tofu, wash in cold running water. Refrigerate, covered with water, in an air-tight container. If the water is changed 2 to 3 times a week, tofu should last from 3 to 4 weeks.

There is no substitute for tofu.

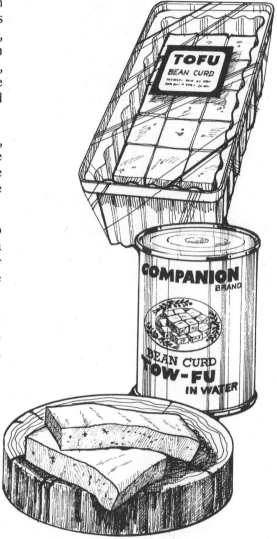

Water Chestnuts

In America most people recognise water chestnuts by their white flesh and moist, crunchy texture as they are prepared in a variety of Chinese dishes.

In China, however, fresh water chestnuts are also a favorite treat eaten raw. The dark brown outer skin is peeled off and the succulent, sweet meat eaten like fruit. (Unfortunately, when canned, water chestnuts lose much of their flavor and sweetness.) About the size of walnuts, fresh water chestnuts are available in oriental markets. They will last up to two weeks if unpeeled and refrigerated. Once peeled, they must be submerged immediately in cold water to prevent discoloration. Peeled Jerusalem artichokes, sun chokes or jicama may be substituted for fresh water chestnuts.

Canned water chestnuts may also be substituted for fresh ones; they are available throughout the United States in oriental markets and most supermarkets. You may find them packed diced, sliced or whole; select the whole chestnuts for the best flavor. Store leftover canned water chestnuts covered in water in an airtight container in the refrigerator. They will last up to one week if the water is changed daily.

Appetizers, Soups and Salads

We think of appetizers, soups and salads as specific courses during a meal. In Chinese cuisine, however, they are served quite differently. The cold appetizers are artfully arranged on a large platter and presented as a cold plate while guests are being seated at the table. Hot appetizers can appear anytime during the dinner. Light soups may be served at the beginning or they may be sipped throughout the meal. Heavier soups can be presented along with other entrée dishes or as a marvelous one-dish lunch. Chinese salads can be served as part of the cold plate or during the meal as a vegetable. These salads are not the tossed greens with which we are familiar but rather cold cooked vegetables with a soy dressing.

You will enjoy serving the following selections as part of a Chinese dinner but there is no reason why you cannot fit them into your everyday family meal planning and party festivities.

Crunchy Radishes

Have these appetizers ready to serve your guests as they watch the preparations of a Chinese dinner.

2 bunches red radishes, washed and trimmed
½ teaspoon salt
2 tablespoons rice wine vinegar or distilled white vinegar
3 tablespoons sugar
5 drops sesame oil

With the broad side of a cleaver or a meat mallet, gently crack radishes and set aside. In a bowl or other container with a tight-fitting lid, combine salt, vinegar and sugar, stirring until sugar is dissolved. Add radishes, cover and shake gently. Refrigerate for 4 to 5 hours, or overnight, gently mixing or shaking occasionally. To serve, drain radishes and sprinkle with sesame oil; toss lightly.

A colorful appetizer to make ahead of time. You'll love crisp, fresh broccoli served this way with its tart vinegar dressing.

Pickled Broccoli

1 pound broccoli
½ teaspoon salt
2 tablespoons sugar
2 tablespoons rice wine vinegar or
     distilled white vinegar
4 drops sesame oil

Wash broccoli and separate stems from flowerettes. If very thick, cut stems in half lengthwise. Peel stems and cut diagonally in ¼ inch slices. Cut flowerettes into bite-size pieces. In a bowl or other container with a tight-fitting lid, mix together salt, sugar, and vinegar until sugar dissolves. Add broccoli and cover tightly. Shake once or twice and refrigerate for at least 1 hour or overnight. Shake or mix occasionally. To serve, drain and sprinkle with sesame oil; toss lightly.

The Cold Plate

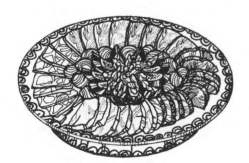

Traditionally, the cold plate is brought to the table to signal the beginning of a festive Chinese banquet. However, you may wish to serve it as part of a party buffet. To prepare this dramatic appetizer, choose a large platter or serving tray and on it create an attractive and colorful food arrangement. Choose a combination of components, such as Crunchy Radishes, Pickled Broccoli, Fresh Vegetable Salad or Chicken Salad plus cold, sliced Red-Cooked Beef, cold Red-Cooked Chicken and, perhaps, Tea Eggs. The cold plate can be prepared hours ahead of time, covered with plastic wrap and kept refrigerated until ready to serve.

Try these red-cooked chicken wings. They are slowly simmered in soy sauce until the sauce thickens and glazes the meat with a deep, red color. Serve them as an appetizer or as part of a meal. They are delicious hot or cold.

Shanghai Chicken Wings

2   pounds chicken drummettes *or* 2½ pounds chicken wings
3   tablespoons sugar
⅓   cup dark soy sauce
⅓   cup water
1   tablespoon Chinese rice wine or dry sherry
    Peanut oil
    Seasonings, one or more of the following:
      1 clove garlic, smashed and minced
      2 slices ginger root, smashed and minced
      2 whole star anise *or* ½ teaspoon five spice powder

PREPARATION: Rinse chicken in cold water and pat dry. If using wings, remove and discard small tips and cut at the joint. Set aside. In a small bowl, combine sugar, soy sauce, water and wine. Set aside. Have peanut oil at hand. Select and prepare seasonings. Set aside.

METHOD: If using garlic or ginger, heat 1 tablespoon oil until it smokes in a dutch oven or other heavy pot with a tight-fitting lid. Add garlic or ginger and sauté until you detect the aroma. Add remaining ingredients. Stir to combine, bring to a boil, cover and simmer for 20 to 25 minutes, stirring occasionally to coat chicken pieces in sauce. Uncover and cook over medium heat 20 to 25 minutes or until chicken is tender and sauce is a dark brown glaze, stirring once or twice to coat chicken. Watch carefully so that chicken does not burn. Remove to a serving dish and discard star anise.

Drunken Chicken

Drunken Chicken is so called because of the wine used for marinating it. It is a favorite dish because it is so easy to prepare and can be made ahead of time.

2½   cups water
1   chicken breast (about 1 lb.)
1   green onion, cut into 2 inch lengths
2   slices ginger root
½   teaspoon salt
½   cup Chinese rice wine or dry sherry
    Condiments: Szechwan pepper-salt (see page 37), chopped cilantro, hoisin sauce, oyster sauce, Chinese hot mustard, soy sauce

In a saucepan, bring water to a boil and add chicken, green onion and ginger. Cover and simmer for 10 minutes. Remove from heat and let stand, covered, for 10 minutes. Drain, reserving broth for other uses; discard ginger and onion pieces. When cool enough to handle, skin and bone chicken placing meat in a small bowl with a tight-fitting lid. Sprinkle lightly with salt and add wine. Cover bowl and refrigerate overnight or several days, stirring occasionally. Just before serving, cut chicken into bite-size pieces and serve with several of the suggested condiments.

You will find Chinese sausages in oriental markets. They are usually made of pork and have a suggestion of sweetness. Use the sausages as an appetizer or steam them with rice, see page 107. Either way, you'll love their truly unique flavor.

Chinese Sausage Appetizer

Chinese sausages
Condiments:
    Chinese hot mustard (see recipe
    below)
    Dijon mustard
    Oyster sauce
    Hoisin sauce

Rinse sausages in water. In wok or other pan equipped for steaming, bring 2 or 3 cups water to a vigorous boil. Place sausages on steam plate, in a heatproof dish or a bamboo steamer. Cover and steam sausages for 15 to 18 minutes. Remove sausages, drain well and slice diagonally into bite-size pieces. Arrange condiments in small sauce dishes and serve sausages with toothpicks.

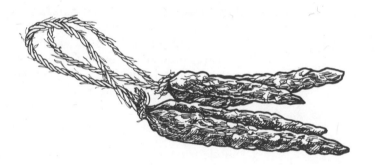

Chinese Hot Mustard

Dry mustard powder
Water

In a small bowl measure approximately 1 tablespoon mustard powder. Slowly add enough water to make a thin paste. Allow to stand 15 minutes before serving. This mustard cannot be stored. Make just enough for immediate use.

Everyone loves these curried turnovers! Serve them warm at luncheon with soup or salad. Take them along on picnics. Although the Chinese make them with a lard based pastry, here is an easy interpretation using crescent rolls or pie crust mix.

Curried Beef Turnovers   *Makes 16 luncheon or 36 appetizer turnovers*

Filling:

- ½   pound lean ground beef
- 1   tablespoon peanut oil
- ¼   cup minced celery
- 1   medium-size carrot, finely grated
- 2   teaspoons sugar
- 3   tablespoons catsup
- 2   teaspoons curry powder
- ½   teaspoon salt
- 2   green onions, minced
- 2   packages refrigerated crescent rolls *or* 1 (11 oz.) package pie crust mix
- 1   egg, lightly beaten

In a large frying pan, brown ground beef in oil. Add celery, carrot, sugar, catsup, curry powder and salt, stirring to combine. Simmer 3 to 4 minutes, add green onion and stir to combine. Remove from heat and allow to cool. Filling mixture may be prepared ahead of time and refrigerated up to 4 or 5 days.

To make luncheon size turnovers, use 2 packages refrigerated crescent rolls. Very carefully remove crescent rolls from tube, making sure not to pull apart or squeeze them. In each package there are two sections; separate these and lay them side by side on a bread board. (If dough seems sticky, flour it lightly.) Pinch together all the diagonal perforations. You will have two rectangles 3-1/2 by 14 inches. Cut each in half along the center perforation and then each piece in half again so that from each tube you have 8 pieces of dough 3-1/2 by 3-1/2 inches. Place 1 rounded tablespoon curried beef filling on each square, brush edges with beaten egg, fold over into a triangle and press to seal edges tightly. Place turnovers on an ungreased baking sheet, brush tops with beaten egg and bake at 375° for 12 to 15 minutes or until brown.

To make appetizer size turnovers, use 1 package pie crust mix. Prepare mix according to package directions. Divide dough into quarters. Roll each quarter into a 7-1/2 inch square, trimming off uneven edges. Cut into nine 2-1/2 inch squares. Place 1 rounded teaspoon curried beef filling at the center of each square and brush edges with beaten egg. Fold crust over diagonally and press to seal tightly. Place turnover on ungreased baking sheet, brush with beaten egg and bake at 375° for 15 minutes, or until golden brown.

Filled, baked turnovers may be frozen. To serve, place frozen turnovers on baking sheet and bake 10 to 15 minutes at 350° or until thawed and warm.

Include this delicious appetizer at your next party. It's an easy choice to prepare—especially with a food processor. And Shrimp Toast can be made early and reheated just before serving.

Shrimp Toast *Makes 32 wedges*

2   green onions, minced
6   water chestnuts, chopped very
     fine
½   pound shrimp, shelled, deveined,
     washed and dried, very
     finely minced
     Ginger root, smashed and
     minced, enough to make
     1 teaspoon
1¼ teaspoons salt
½   teaspoon sugar
1   teaspoon Chinese rice wine or
     dry sherry
1   egg, slightly beaten
1   tablespoon cornstarch
8   slices dried white bread,
     trimmed of all crusts
2   cups peanut oil, for deep-
     frying

PREPARATION: *To make filling by hand,* combine minced green onions, chopped water chestnuts and finely minced shrimp in a bowl. Add ginger, salt, sugar, wine, egg and cornstarch. Blend thoroughly.

If using a food processor, cut onions into 2 inch lengths and quarter water chestnuts. Put onion pieces into work bowl with steel knife in place and quickly turn processor on and off 2 or 3 times. Add water chestnuts and quickly turn processor on and off 2 or 3 times. Add whole shrimp and quickly turn processor on and off 2 or 3 times. Add ginger, salt, sugar, wine, egg and cornstarch. Quickly turn processor on and off 2 or 3 times to blend. Do not over-process; mixture should still be slightly chunky. If desired, shrimp mixture may be made ahead to this point and refrigerated for 2 to 3 days.

METHOD: Spread shrimp mixture evenly over bread, spreading it right to the edges. In a wok or other deep-frying pan, heat oil to 375° or until a cube of bread dropped into the oil rises to the surface and browns quickly. Place 1 or 2 pieces prepared bread *shrimp side down* in oil and fry for 30 to 60 seconds, until edges are brown. Turn over and brown the other side, about 5 to 6 seconds. Remove toast from oil and drain on tempura rack or paper towels. Repeat until all pieces are fried. Just before serving, cut each slice diagonally into triangular quarters. Serve warm.

Shrimp Toast may be fried a few hours before serving. To reheat, place toast on baking sheet in a 350° oven for 10 to 15 minutes. Cut into serving pieces.

A light Chinese soup is a refreshing way to begin a meal. Here are several favorites that you can make quickly and easily. If you do not have homemade broth on hand, simply use canned broth or bouillon.

Egg Flower Soup *Serves 4 to 6*

1 egg
½ teaspoon salt
1 tablespoon cornstarch
2 tablespoons cold water
3 cups chicken broth
½ cup green peas, fresh or frozen
½ teaspoon ginger juice (see page 66) *or* 1 slice ginger root
2 teaspoons Chinese rice wine or dry sherry
1 green onion, finely chopped
Sesame oil (optional)

In a small bowl, beat egg lightly with salt. Set aside. In another small bowl, combine cornstarch and water. Set aside. In a saucepan, bring chicken broth to boiling. Add cornstarch mixture, lower heat and simmer until clear. Add peas, ginger juice and wine. Simmer for 1 minute. Very slowly, pour beaten egg mixture into soup. With a chopstick in the other hand, make wide circles on the surface of the soup to catch the egg and draw it into long, filmy threads. (If using ginger root, remove it before serving.) Ladle soup into large soup bowl, tureen or 4 to 6 individual soup bowls. Serve at once garnished with green onions and few drops of sesame oil.

Clear Chicken Soup with Sole and Vegetables *Serves 4 to 6*

4 cups chicken broth
4 fresh mushrooms, sliced
1 head iceberg lettuce, cored and shredded
4 teaspoons light soy sauce
¾ cup filet of sole or any delicate white fish, sliced very thin across the grain
Sesame oil (optional)

In a saucepan, bring chicken broth to a boil and add mushrooms and lettuce. Bring to a boil again, add soy sauce and fish. Remove from heat at once; stir gently. Ladle into large soup bowl, tureen or 4 to 6 individual soup bowls. Garnish with a few drops of sesame oil. Serve immediately.

Bamboo Shoot, Green Pepper and Ginger Soup *Serves 4*

1   small green bell pepper,
       shredded and blanched
       3 minutes
     Bamboo shoot, shredded,
       about ½ cup
4   cups chicken broth
1   large slice ginger root, slightly
       smashed

Distribute green pepper and bamboo shoot evenly among 4 individual soup bowls or place in a large soup bowl or tureen. In a saucepan, heat chicken broth with ginger until boiling. Remove ginger slice and pour broth over vegetables. Serve immediately.

Fresh green beans may be substituted for green pepper. Cut beans into 2 inch lengths and julienne. Blanch for 2 minutes.

Soup's On

To add to the fun and authenticity of your Chinese dinner, you may want to set the table with individual Chinese soup bowls and flat-bottomed porcelain soup spoons. (The bowls may be used also as rice bowls.) Present the soup in a large Chinese soup bowl with its porcelain serving spoon. These bowls are made in many colorful designs and are available in oriental shops or you may find them in import specialty stores across the country.

There are two types of won ton soup. One is served as a first-course and is a popular restaurant item. It consists of a clear, thin broth, a few won ton, perhaps a few pieces of spinach, a few peas or just a green onion garnish. It is a light, delicious way to begin a meal. At home, however, Chinese families often serve a won ton soup as the whole meal. This soup has 6 to 10 won ton per person plus vegetables, shrimp or thin slices of pork or chicken, strips of egg and perhaps other tidbits, all garnished with green onion.

First Course Won Ton Soup   *Serves 4*

4   cups chicken broth
1   tablespoon light soy sauce
20   filled Won Ton (see pages 115-117),
       boiled, steamed or deep-fried
¼   cup green peas, fresh or frozen *or*
       1 cup fresh spinach leaves,
       torn into bite-size pieces
2   green onions, minced

In a large saucepan, heat broth and soy sauce to boiling. Add won ton and simmer for 2 to 3 minutes. Add peas and simmer to heat through. Garnish with green onions and ladle into a large soup bowl, tureen or 4 individual soup bowls. Serve at once.

Full Meal Won Ton Soup   *Serves 3 to 4*

1   egg sheet (see recipe), cut into
       ½ inch strips
4   cups chicken broth
30   filled Won Ton (see pages
       115-117), boiled, steamed
       or deep-fried
½   cup sliced bamboo shoots
4   soaked dried black mushrooms
       (see page 28), sliced
1   cup spinach, cut into ¾ inch
       pieces
8   shrimp, shelled, deveined,
       washed and dried *or*
       ½ to 1 cup leftover cooked
       meat
2   green onions, shredded
       Soy sauce or salt
       Pepper

PREPARATION: Prepare egg sheet and cut into strips. Place chicken broth in a large saucepan and set aside. Have cooked won ton ready to add as needed. On a platter arrange prepared bamboo shoots, mushrooms, spinach, shrimp, egg strips, and green onions. Set aside. Have soy sauce and pepper at hand.

METHOD: Bring chicken broth to a boil; add won ton, bamboo shoots, mushrooms and shrimp. Bring to a boil and add spinach. Reheat to boiling and add egg strips. Season to taste with soy sauce and pepper. Ladle into large soup bowl, tureen or individual bowls, garnish with green onions and serve piping hot.

Egg Sheet: In a small bowl, beat together 1 egg, 1 teaspoon dry sherry and a pinch of salt. Heat a small (8 to 10-inch) frying pan and add 1 teaspoon oil. Rotate pan to spread oil evenly over surface. Pour in egg mixture, rotate pan to make a thin pancake and cook until the underside of pancake is a light brown. Remove egg sheet from pan and let cool. When cool enough to handle, roll up egg sheet like a jelly roll and cut into 1/2 inch slices.

Hot and Sour Soup is a dish served by the Chinese at home to the family. It is not considered company fare. However, its delicious combination of flavors has made it a favorite selection in restaurants. For a memorable supper, make this hearty version and serve it with warm French bread.

Hot and Sour Soup *Serves 4 to 6*

¼ pound lean pork butt, sliced
1 teaspoon cornstarch
3 tablespoons light soy sauce
1 slice ginger root, smashed and minced
4 soaked dried black mushrooms (see page 28), sliced
1 cup shredded celery cabbage
½ cup green peas, fresh or frozen
Bamboo shoots, shredded, about ½ cup
1 cake Chinese-style tofu, pressed and cut into matchstick-size pieces
2 green onions, minced
1 egg, slightly beaten
4 cups chicken broth
1 tablespoon peanut oil
2 tablespoons rice wine vinegar or white distilled vinegar
¼ teaspoon white pepper
Salt
Sesame oil
Chinese hot oil (optional)

PREPARATION: In a small bowl, combine sliced pork with cornstarch, 1 tablespoon soy sauce and ginger. Set aside for 15 to 20 minutes. On a platter arrange prepared mushrooms, celery cabbage, peas, bamboo shoots, tofu and green onions. Set aside. In a small bowl, lightly beat egg and set aside. Have chicken broth, peanut oil, vinegar, pepper, salt, sesame oil and hot oil ready to add as needed.

METHOD: Heat wok and add 1 tablespoon peanut oil. With spatula, swirl oil to coat sides of wok and heat until oil just begins to smoke. Add pork, spreading it in a single layer, and stir-fry briefly, about 30 seconds. Add mushrooms, celery cabbage, bamboo shoots and peas. Continue to stir-fry 2 to 3 minutes. Add broth, bring to a simmer, cover and simmer for 5 to 6 minutes. Add 2 tablespoons soy sauce, vinegar and tofu pieces. Continue to simmer 1 to 2 minutes. Add pepper and salt to taste. Slowly pour in beaten egg. With a chopstick in the other hand, make wide circles on the surface of the soup to catch the egg and draw it into long, filmy threads. Add a few drops of hot oil and sesame oil. Ladle into a large bowl, tureen or 4 to 6 individual soup bowls. Serve at once garnished with green onions.

Chinese Hot Oil (Chili Oil)

Chinese hot oil adds a delicious fiery flavor to foods. It is used in cooking and as an ingredient in dipping sauces. You can buy bottles of hot oil in oriental markets or make your own.

1 cup peanut oil (or other vegetable oil)
1 ounce dried red chile peppers

In a deep stainless steel or Corningware pan, heat oil over medium heat until it just begins to smoke. Remove from heat, add chiles and allow to stand overnight. Next day, strain oil into a glass container with a tight-fitting lid and seal. Hot oil will last indefinitely.

The Mongolian Hot Pot

One of the handsomest cooking vessels of any cuisine is the Mongolian Hot Pot (or Fire Pot). Made of copper, brass or aluminum, this unique pot features a chimney at the center which is surrounded by a bowl. Charcoal is placed in the chimney and ignited; soup or broth is poured into the bowl and heated by the burning charcoal throughout the meal. The food is cooked right at the table.

The Mongolian Hot Pot originated ages ago on the Asian steppes, where nomadic tribes would gather around a fire and cook their food on skewers in a bubbling cauldron of broth. Gradually this cooking method was introduced to the Northern Chinese. Today, the Hot Pot recipes are found throughout China with surprising regional variations.

The Mongolian Hot Pot dinner is a festive occasion. With the hot pot at the center, guests are seated at the table and prepare their own dipping sauces from various condiments. A platter of thinly sliced meats, fish and vegetables is offered. As the soup simmers in the Hot Pot, the guests pick up tidbits of food with their chopsticks or with wire mesh scoops and cook the food quickly in the broth. When the food is cooked, it is dipped in the condiment sauce and eaten. When all the food is consumed, the remaining broth is poured into soup bowls, mixed with any remaining dipping sauce and the embellished broth is sipped to end a memorable meal.

Although the Mongolian Pot is the authentic utensil for this meal, there is no reason why you cannot accomplish this dinner with an electric deep fryer, an electric wok or any electric cooking pan that will keep the broth at a constant simmer.

Recipes for the Mongolian Hot Pot vary from a preference for lamb in the North to chicken and pork in the South. The Chrysanthemum Hot Pot recipe calls for floating petals to simmer in the broth. The Ten Varieties recipe consists of ingredients already cooked in the broth and selected by the guests throughout the meal. This recipe offers classic flavors you'll love to prepare again and again.

Mongolian Hot Pot Dinner   *Serves 6 to 8*

1   chicken breast (about 1½ lbs.), skinned, boned and sliced

1   pound filet mignon or flank steak, sliced

¾   pound shrimp, shelled, deveined, washed, dried and butterflied

1   head celery cabbage (about 1 lb.), cut into bite-size pieces or fresh spinach leaves

2   cakes Chinese-style tofu, pressed and cut into 1 inch cubes

2   ounces cellophane noodles, softened in boiling water for 5 minutes and well drained

2   quarts chicken broth
      Condiments, for dipping sauce
      light soy sauce
      shredded green onions
      Chinese rice wine or dry sherry
      shredded ginger root
      sesame oil
      Chinese hot oil
      chopped cilantro

PREPARATION: Arrange prepared chicken, beef, shrimp, celery cabbage, tofu and cellophane noodles on serving platter. In a saucepan, bring chicken broth to a boil. Have condiments in individual bowls at the table. Wrap a heavy chopping block or bread board with aluminum foil and place in the center of the dinner table. Set the Hot Pot on the block, filled with charcoal ready to ignite. Set each place setting with a soup bowl for dipping sauce and a small wire mesh scoop and chopsticks.

METHOD: Before guests are assembled at the table, pour hot chicken broth into Hot Pot and ignite charcoal. When broth is simmering, call guests to the table. Allow each guest to mix his own dipping sauce from assorted condiments. Place platter of prepared foods on the table and let guests help themselves, placing pieces one at a time in hot broth with scoop or chopsticks until cooked and then dipping them in sauce.

When all food is eaten, carefully ladle broth into bowls, combine with any dipping sauce remaining in bowl, and sip.

You will enjoy the way colors, textures and flavors are combined in Chinese salads. The crispy Vegetable Salad is tossed with a soy-vinegar dressing. The Chicken Salad dressing is hot and spicy. Both salads are customarily served at room temperature but you could chill them if you wish.

Chinese Chicken Salad *Serves 6 to 8*

1	chicken breast (about 1 lb.) Water, about 2 to 3 cups
¼	pound bean sprouts, blanched 1 minute and thoroughly drained
1	large cucumber, thinly sliced
2	tablespoons light soy sauce
1½	tablespoons rice wine vinegar or white distilled vinegar
1	teaspoon ginger juice (see page 66) *or* 1 small slice ginger root, smashed and minced
1	teaspoon sugar
1	teaspoon Chinese hot oil *or* 1 tablespoon chili paste *or* ½ teaspoon Tabasco sauce
1	clove garlic, smashed and minced
½	teaspoon salt
½	teaspoon pepper
1	teaspoon dry mustard
¼	cup minced green onion
¼	cup fresh cilantro, chopped
1	tablespoon sesame oil Deep-fried rice sticks (see recipe) about 2 small handfuls *or* ¼ cup toasted sesame seeds

PREPARATION: Cut chicken breast in half. In a saucepan, bring 2 to 3 cups water to a boil. Add chicken and bring to a second boil. Cover, remove from heat and let stand for 20 to 25 minutes. Drain chicken (reserving broth for other uses) and let cool. When cool enough to handle, skin and bone chicken, shredding meat into long thin pieces. (Skin may also be sliced and added to meat.) Set aside. Add bean sprouts to chicken and set aside. Prepare cucumber and set aside. In a small bowl, combine soy sauce, vinegar, ginger juice, sugar, Chinese hot oil, garlic, salt, pepper and mustard. Stir to dissolve sugar and salt completely. Set aside. In a small bowl, combine prepared green onion and cilantro. Have sesame oil and fried rice sticks at hand. (If desired, dish may be made ahead to this point and set aside until ready to serve.)

METHOD: To assemble, combine chicken, bean sprouts and crushed, fried rice sticks in a large bowl. Add soy sauce dressing and sesame oil. Toss to combine. On a serving platter, lay cucumber slices in an even layer and top with chicken mixture. Garnish with green onion and cilantro. Serve salad at room temperature.

Variations: a) Blend 2 tablespoons chunky peanut butter into soy dressing
 b) Add 1/2 cup shredded barbecue pork or ham to chicken

To deep-fry rice sticks, heat 2 cups peanut oil in wok to 375° or until a cube of bread dropped in oil rises to the surface and browns quickly. Add 1 small handful rice sticks and let cook for about 5 seconds or until rice sticks have puffed. Turn sticks with bamboo tongs to fry all rice sticks and remove from oil; drain on tempura rack or paper towel.

Fresh Vegetable Salad   *Serves 4 to 6*

½   pound bean sprouts, washed and
    drained thoroughly
2   cups shredded celery cabbage
6   fresh mushrooms, sliced *or*
    8 red radishes, sliced
3   tablespoons light soy sauce
2   tablespoons rice wine vinegar or
    white distilled vinegar
1   tablespoon salad oil
2   tablespoons sugar
1   teaspoon salt
1   tablespoon sesame oil

Combine prepared bean sprouts, celery cabbage and mushrooms in a salad bowl. Set aside. In a small bowl, combine soy sauce, vinegar, salad oil, sugar and salt, stirring until sugar and salt are completely dissolved. (If desired, dish may be made ahead to this point and refrigerated until ready to serve.) Add sesame oil to dressing. Pour dressing over vegetables and toss to combine.

Make the Most of Green Onions

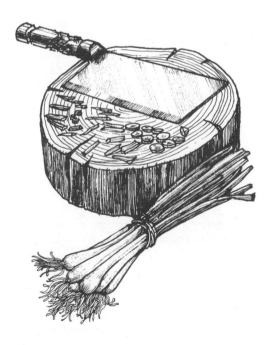

Green onions (also called scallions) are as popular in China as in other countries around the world. The delicate flavor of green onions and their fresh spring color are employed in countless Chinese dishes as a garnish and condiment.

Bunches of green onions are available year round at your local supermarket. To store, wrap them in plastic wrap and place in the crisper section of your refrigerator. If fresh, green onions will keep up to 1 week.

In Chinese cooking, almost the entire green onion is prepared, including most of the green stalk. Remove only bruised or dried ends and the roots. Place the green onion on a cutting board and, with the broad side of the cleaver blade, give one sharp, light blow to the white end of the onion. This will flatten it and prevent pieces from rolling while you slice or mince.

If green onions are unavailable, use finely minced yellow, white or red onion for the flavor. Green peas, parsley or cilantro will provide the same colorful accent as a green onion garnish.

Tea Eggs are usually served as an appetizer. You may cut the eggs in halves or quarters and arrange them on a serving plate, or you may arrange them as part of a cold plate.

Tea Eggs   *Makes 12 eggs*

1   dozen small eggs, hard cooked
1   quart boiling water
5   tea bags *or* 3 tablespoons orange
        pekoe tea
2   whole star anise
4   tablespoons light soy sauce
1   teaspoon peanut oil *or* sesame oil

To prepare eggs, follow either of two methods:

1) Shell cooked eggs very carefully, being sure not to break the egg white. Set aside. In a kettle or bowl, pour boiling water over tea bags and allow to steep for 5 to 8 minutes. Strain tea into a large stainless steel saucepan. Add star anise, soy sauce and eggs. Simmer, uncovered, for 1 hour. Remove from heat and set aside to cool. Place eggs with liquid in a bowl and add oil. Cover and chill until ready to serve. Drain just before serving. Eggs will resemble huge black olives. If covered and refrigerated, eggs will keep in liquid for 2 to 3 days.

2) This method gives the eggs a lovely crackled pattern. With the back of a spoon, gently crack eggshells all over but do not remove them. Prepare tea as directed above and strain into a large stainless steel saucepan. Add star anise, soy sauce and eggs. Simmer, uncovered, for 1 hour. Remove from heat and set aside to cool. When cool enough to handle, shell eggs. Place eggs with liquid in a bowl, add oil; cover and chill until ready to serve. Drain just before serving. If covered and refrigerated, eggs will keep in liquid for 2 to 3 days.

Beef, Pork and Lamb Dishes

When the Chinese cook meat it is often stir-fried in combination with a variety of vegetables. Thus a minimum of meat will serve more people. You will appreciate this budget-saving economy! You'll also like the convenience of preparing meats and vegetables together. (By adding a little broth, you can serve most of these stir-fry recipes over rice for a quick and easy one-dish supper.)

Along with this great gathering of stir-fry dishes, you'll find slowly simmered red-cooked favorites, two versions of Mu Shu Pork, a delicious barbecued pork and an unforgettable saté.

Stir-Fry Beef with Green Peppers *Serves 3 to 4 American style, 4 to 6 Chinese style*

A typical Cantonese dish consists of meat stir-fried with vegetables, lightly seasoned. Succulent beef combined with tender crisp green peppers and celery is one delicious example.

1 pound beef flank steak, cut into ½ inch cubes *or* 1 pound sirloin steak, cut into ¾ inch cubes
4 tablespoons light soy sauce
2 tablespoons Chinese rice wine or dry sherry
1 teaspoon sugar
Peanut oil
2 green bell peppers, cut into 1 inch wedges
1 rib celery, cut into 1 inch wedges
Salt
Water

PREPARATION: In a small bowl, combine steak cubes with 2 tablespoons soy sauce, wine, sugar and 1 teaspoon oil. Set aside for 15 to 20 minutes. On a platter, arrange prepared green peppers and celery. Set aside. Have remaining 2 tablespoons soy sauce, oil, salt and water ready to add as needed.

METHOD: Heat wok and add 1 tablespoon oil. With a spatula, swirl oil to coat sides of wok and heat until oil just begins to smoke. Add celery, stir-fry briefly, add a pinch of salt and sprinkle 1 tablespoon water down sides of wok. Stir-fry until tender crisp, about 2 minutes. Remove from wok and set aside. To wok add 1 tablespoon oil and heat until oil just begins to smoke. Add green pepper, stir-fry briefly, add a pinch of salt and sprinkle 1 tablespoon water down sides. Stir-fry until tender crisp, about 2 minutes. Remove from wok and set aside. To wok add 2 tablespoons oil and heat until oil just begins to smoke. Add beef, spreading it in a single layer and stir-fry 3 to 4 minutes. Return vegetables to wok and stir-fry to combine. Add 2 tablespoons soy sauce and stir-fry to combine. Remove to serving dish and serve at once.

Ginger, one of the most important ingredients in Chinese cooking, is very pronounced in some dishes. Here it is accented in the popular stir-fry beef and onion combination.

Stir-Fry Ginger Beef *Serves 3 to 4 American style, 4 to 6 Chinese style*

1   pound beef flank steak, sliced
4   teaspoons cornstarch
2   tablespoons light soy sauce
3   teaspoons Chinese rice wine or
        dry sherry
1   teaspoon sugar
     Peanut oil
1   medium-size onion, cut into
        eighths with the grain
     Ginger root, smashed and minced,
        enough to make 3 tablespoons
1   small clove garlic, smashed and
        minced
2   tablespoons oyster sauce
     Beef or chicken broth, ¾ to
        1 cup
     Salt
     Water

PREPARATION: In a small bowl, combine sliced flank steak, 2 teaspoons cornstarch, soy sauce, 2 teaspoons wine, 1/2 teaspoon sugar and 1 tablespoon oil. Set aside for 15 to 20 minutes. On a platter, arrange prepared onion, ginger and garlic. Set aside. In a bowl, blend oyster sauce, 1/2 teaspoon sugar, 1 teaspoon wine, 2 teaspoons cornstarch and 1/2 cup broth. Have remaining broth, oil, salt and water ready to add as needed.

METHOD: Heat wok and add 1 tablespoon oil. With spatula, swirl oil around to coat sides of wok and heat until oil just begins to smoke. Add onions, stir-fry briefly and add a pinch of salt. Sprinkle 1 tablespoon water down sides of wok and stir-fry until onions are tender crisp, about 2 to 3 minutes. Remove onions from wok and set aside. To wok add 3 tablespoons oil and heat until oil just begins to smoke. Add ginger and garlic and stir-fry until golden brown. Add beef, spreading it in a single layer and stir-fry for 1 to 2 minutes. Return onions to wok and stir-fry to combine. Make a well and add oyster sauce mixture. Stir-fry to combine. If serving this dish American style over rice, you will want more liquid; add remaining broth and stir-fry until heated through. Remove to serving dish and serve at once.

One of the most luxurious and easiest of stir-fry dishes uses filet mignon tossed with snow peas, bamboo shoots and celery cabbage. When you want to make a dazzling impression, serve this.

Stir-Fry Steak Kew *Serves 3 to 4 American style, 6 to 8 Chinese style*

1	pound filet mignon or other very tender beef steak, well trimmed and cut into 1 inch chunks
1	tablespoon oyster sauce
2	tablespoons light soy sauce
2	tablespoons Chinese rice wine or dry sherry
½	teaspoon sugar
1	teaspoon cornstarch
¼	teaspoon pepper
1	cup snow peas, fresh or frozen
1	clove garlic, smashed and minced
2	slices ginger root, smashed and minced
8	soaked dried black mushrooms (see page 28), halved *or* 8 fresh mushrooms, quartered
1	onion, cut into 1 inch wedges
½	cup sliced bamboo shoots
	Celery cabbage, cut into 1 inch wedges, enough to make 1 cup
	Peanut oil
	Salt

PREPARATION: In a bowl, combine filet pieces, oyster sauce, soy sauce, wine, sugar, cornstarch and pepper. Set aside for 15 to 20 minutes. If using fresh snow peas, remove stems and strings and soak in ice water for 15 minutes. If using frozen snow peas, have them defrosted. On a large platter, arrange prepared snow peas, garlic, ginger, mushrooms, onion, bamboo shoots and celery cabbage. Have oil and salt ready to add as needed.

METHOD: Heat wok and add 2 tablespoons peanut oil. With spatula, swirl oil to coat sides of wok and heat until oil just begins to smoke. Add meat and quickly stir-fry to sear meat on all sides. Work very fast so that meat cooks only 1 minute. Remove meat from wok and set aside. Add 1 tablespoon oil to wok and heat until oil just begins to smoke. Add garlic and ginger; stir-fry until golden brown. Add onion, stir-fry for 10 seconds and add a pinch of salt. Stir-fry for 1 to 2 minutes. Add bamboo shoots, celery cabbage and mushrooms. Stir-fry for 1 to 2 minutes or until tender crisp. Return meat to wok and add snow peas. Cover wok and steam for 1 to 2 minutes, or until snow peas are just tender crisp. Remove to serving plate and serve at once.

One taste of this hot, spicy dish and you'll know why Szechwan cooking has become so popular. (Use the chili paste lightly, you can always add more.) Serve this with rice or with Mandarin pancakes.

Stir-Fry Beef with Chili Paste *Serves 3 to 4 American style, 4 to 6 Chinese style*

1	pound beef flank steak, sliced
2½	tablespoons dark soy sauce
3½	teaspoons cornstarch
1	teaspoon sugar
	Peanut oil
½	cup shredded bamboo shoots, *or* ½ cup shredded carrots
½	cup shredded celery
1	medium-size onion, cut into eighths with the grain
2	cloves garlic, smashed and minced
3	slices ginger root, smashed and minced
½	cup chicken or beef broth
1	teaspoon chili paste
	Salt
	Water

PREPARATION: In a small bowl, combine sliced flank steak, soy sauce, 2-1/2 teaspoons cornstarch, sugar and 1 tablespoon peanut oil. Set aside for 15 to 20 minutes. On a platter, arrange prepared bamboo shoots, celery, onion, garlic and ginger. Set aside. In a small bowl mix together remaining 1 teaspoon cornstarch and broth. Set aside. Have chili paste, additional peanut oil, salt and water ready to use as needed.

METHOD: Heat wok and add 1 tablespoon oil. With a spatula, swirl oil around to coat sides of wok and heat until oil just begins to smoke. Add bamboo shoots, stir-fry briefly. Add a pinch of salt and pour 1 tablespoon water down sides of wok. Continue to stir-fry 1 minute. Remove from wok and set aside. To wok add 1 tablespoon oil and heat until oil just begins to smoke. Add celery and stir-fry 1 minute. Add onion, a pinch of salt and a tablespoon of water. Stir-fry until tender crisp, about 2 to 3 minutes. Remove from wok and set aside. To wok add 2-1/2 tablespoons oil and heat until oil just begins to smoke. Add ginger and garlic, stir-frying until golden brown. Add beef, spreading it in a single layer, and stir-fry for 2 to 3 minutes. Add chili paste and stir-fry briefly. Return vegetables to wok and stir-fry to combine. Make a well and add broth mixture; stir-fry until heated through. Remove to a serving plate and serve at once.

Here's a marvelous introduction to red-cooking. Beef simmered in soy sauce with the added flavor of star anise. Serve it hot with its own sauce or cold as part of a cold plate.

Red-Cooked Beef   *Serves 4 to 6 American style, 8 to 10 Chinese style*

2   pounds beef pot roast, bottom round, chuck roast or very meaty short ribs
3   slices ginger root, smashed and minced
1   large clove garlic, smashed and minced
¼   cup dark soy sauce
3   tablespoons Chinese rice wine or dry sherry
1   tablespoon sugar
1   teaspoon salt
1   cup hot tap water
     Peanut oil
2   whole star anise
1   piece fresh orange peel, about ¼ by 2 inches

PREPARATION: Trim beef of excess fat and pat dry. Set aside. Mince ginger and garlic and set aside. In a small bowl, combine soy sauce, wine, sugar and salt. Set aside. Have hot tap water, oil, star anise and orange peel at hand.

METHOD: In a heavy, ovenproof pan or casserole with a tight-fitting lid, heat 2 tablespoons oil until oil just begins to smoke. Add garlic and ginger and sauté until you detect the aroma. Add beef and brown on all sides. Add soy sauce mixture, orange peel and star anise. Pour hot tap water around edges of pan and bring to a boil. Cover and place pan in 350° oven and bake for 3 to 4 hours, or until meat is very tender and cooked through. Remove meat from casserole and allow to stand for 15 minutes. Cut into thin slices or cubes. Strain sauce and remove any excess grease with a bulb baster or paper towel. Serve beef accompanied with sauce.

To serve chilled as an appetizer or as part of a cold plate (see page 41), transfer meat and strained, defatted sauce to another container, cover and refrigerate. Before serving, cut meat into 2 by 2 inch strips and slice very thin. (Save sauce for other uses.)

Here's the easiest Cantonese stir-fry of all. The vegetables are stir-fried and then steamed for a few minutes. The vegetable combinations are endless but here are just a few suggestions.

Stir-Fry Beef with Vegetables   *Serves 3 to 4 American style, 6 to 8 Chinese style*

1 pound beef flank steak, sliced
Cornstarch
2 tablespoons light soy sauce
2 tablespoons Chinese rice wine or dry sherry
½ teaspoon sugar
Peanut oil
Vegetable combination (see below)
2 small slices ginger root, smashed and minced
2 green onions, minced
1 tablespoon water (optional)
½ cup beef or chicken broth
1 teaspoon salt

PREPARATION: In a small bowl, combine sliced flank steak, 2 teaspoons cornstarch, soy sauce, wine, sugar and 1 tablespoon oil. Set aside for 15 to 20 minutes. Prepare selected vegetables and arrange them on a platter with minced ginger and green onions. Set aside. If used, combine 2 teaspoons additional cornstarch and 1 tablespoon water in a small bowl. Set aside. Have broth, salt and oil at hand and ready to add as needed.

METHOD: Heat wok and add 2 tablespoons oil. With a spatula, swirl oil around to coat sides of wok and heat until oil just begins to smoke. Add green onions and ginger and stir-fry until you detect the aroma. Add beef, spreading it in a single layer, and stir-fry 1 to 2 minutes. Remove from wok and set aside. To wok add 1-1/2 tablespoons oil and heat until oil just begins to smoke. Add remaining vegetables on platter and stir-fry briefly. Add 1 teaspoon salt and stir-fry to combine. Make a well and pour in broth. Stir-fry to combine, cover wok and let steam 5 to 7 minutes, or until vegetables are tender crisp. If a thicker sauce is desired, add cornstarch mixture and heat until sauce is clear. Return meat to wok and stir-fry to combine. Remove to serving plate and serve at once.

SUGGESTED VEGETABLE COMBINATIONS:

1)   1 cup sliced bamboo shoots
     2 green peppers, shredded
     4 to 5 soaked dried black mushrooms (see page 28), sliced

2)   1 onion, cut into eighths with the grain
     1 cup fresh mushrooms, sliced
     1 cup celery cabbage or regular cabbage, thinly sliced

3) 1 rib celery, shredded diagonally
    1 cup shredded carrots
    1 to 2 small zucchini squash, sliced diagonally into
    ½ inch pieces

4) 1 cup green peas, fresh or frozen
    1 cup mushrooms, fresh or canned, sliced
    ½ cup sliced water chestnuts

Stir-Fry Curried Beef with Onions *Serves 3 to 4 American style, 6 to 8 Chinese style*

Although curry is native to India, the Chinese use this intriguing blend of spices for variety in some dishes. Here it flavors beef with onions. Serve this dish as part of a Chinese meal or serve it over rice accompanied by a green vegetable and tossed salad. Either way, it's bound to be a family favorite.

1   pound beef flank steak, sliced
    Peanut oil
2   tablespoons light soy sauce
½   teaspoon sugar
3   teaspoons cornstarch
1   teaspoon Chinese rice wine or
    dry sherry
2   large onions, cut into rings and
    separated
2   cloves garlic, smashed and minced
2   slices ginger root, smashed and
    minced
½   cup chicken broth or water
    Curry powder, 1 to 2 tablespoons
½   cup water

PREPARATION: In a bowl, combine sliced flank steak, 1 tablespoon oil, soy sauce, sugar, 1 teaspoon cornstarch and wine. Set aside for 15 to 20 minutes. On a platter, arrange onion rings, garlic and ginger; set aside. In a small bowl, mix together remaining 2 teaspoons cornstarch with 2 tablespoons broth. Set aside. Have additional broth, curry powder, oil and 1/2 cup water ready to add as needed.

METHOD: Heat wok and add 2 tablespoons oil. With spatula, swirl oil to coat sides of wok and heat until oil just begins to smoke. Add garlic and ginger and stir-fry until golden brown. Add steak slices, spreading them in a single layer, and stir-fry about 1 minute. Remove from wok and set aside. Rinse wok with 1/2 cup water, stirring to remove food particles. Pour water into a cup and reserve for sauce mixture. Wipe wok with paper towel. To wok add 1 tablespoon oil and heat until oil just begins to smoke. Add onion rings and stir-fry until onions are golden brown, about 2 to 3 minutes. Add curry powder and continue to stir-fry for an additional 1 to 2 minutes. Return beef to wok and stir-fry to combine. Add cornstarch mixture and gradually pour in reserved pan water. Stir-fry to blend. If serving this dish American style over rice, you will want more liquid. Add additional broth as desired and stir-fry to heat through. Remove to serving dish and serve at once.

Chili paste is used in Szechwan cooking to add a hot, spicy flavor. Without it, this stir-fry beef with oyster sauce and broccoli is a mild dish. Add the chili paste and it becomes a Szechwan classic.

Stir-Fry Beef with Oyster Sauce and Broccoli *Serves 3 to 4 American style, 6 to 8 Chinese style*

1   pound beef flank steak, sliced
3   tablespoons oyster sauce
2½ teaspoons cornstarch
½   teaspoon sugar
    Peanut oil
2   cloves garlic, smashed and minced
2   slices ginger root, smashed and
      minced
2   cups broccoli, flowerettes cut
      into bite-size pieces, stems
      sliced diagonally into ¼ inch
      pieces
4   soaked dried black mushrooms
      (see page 28), sliced *or* 1 (4 oz.)
      can sliced mushrooms, well
      drained and liquid reserved
½   teaspoon chili paste (optional)
½   cup liquid reserved from
      mushrooms
    Salt
    Water

PREPARATION: In a bowl, combine sliced flank steak, oyster sauce, cornstarch, sugar and 1 tablespoon oil. Set aside for 15 to 20 minutes. On a platter, arrange prepared garlic, ginger, broccoli and mushrooms. Set aside. Have chili paste and mushroom liquid measured and ready to add as needed. Have oil, salt and water at hand.

METHOD: Heat wok and add 1 tablespoon oil. With spatula, swirl oil around to coat sides of wok and heat until oil just begins to smoke. Add broccoli stems and a pinch of salt. Stir-fry briefly, about 10 seconds, and sprinkle 1 tablespoon water down sides of wok. Stir-fry for 1 minute; add broccoli flowerettes and continue to stir-fry until tender crisp, about 3 minutes. Remove broccoli from wok and set aside. To wok add 2 tablespoons oil and heat until oil just begins to smoke. Add ginger and garlic and stir-fry until golden brown. Add beef, spreading it in a single layer, and stir fry for 1 minute. Add mushrooms and stir-fry to heat through, about 1 minute. Return broccoli to wok, add chili paste and stir-fry to combine. If serving this dish American style over rice, you will want more liquid. Add up to 1/2 cup liquid reserved from mushrooms. Stir-fry until heated through. Remove to serving dish and serve at once.

Meatballs at their delicious best—slowly simmered in soy sauce. Serve them Chinese style or American style over rice. Your family will ask for encores!

Red-Cooked Meatballs *Makes approximately 30 meatballs*

2	tablespoons light soy sauce
1	teaspoon sugar
4	teaspoons Chinese rice wine or dry sherry
1	whole star anise
1	pound lean ground beef
¼	cup dried bread crumbs
1	tablespoon cornstarch
1	egg
1	cup chicken broth or water
½	teaspoon salt
½	teaspoon pepper
2	cloves garlic, smashed and minced
2	slices ginger root, smashed and minced
1	pound fresh spinach, washed and cut in half (optional)
	Peanut oil
	Salt

PREPARATION: In a small bowl, combine soy sauce, sugar, 2 teaspoons wine and star anise. Set aside. In a bowl, combine beef, bread crumbs, cornstarch, egg, 1/4 cup broth, salt, pepper and 2 teaspoons wine. Blend thoroughly, using hands if necessary. Form into meatballs about the size of a walnut. (If desired, both sauce and meatballs may be made ahead to this point and refrigerated until ready to cook.) Prepare garlic, ginger and spinach. Set aside. Have additional broth, peanut oil and salt at hand.

METHOD: Heat wok and add 2 tablespoons oil. With a spatula, swirl oil around to coat sides of wok and heat until oil just begins to smoke. Add garlic and ginger; stir-fry until golden brown. Add half of the meatballs and brown on all sides. Remove from wok and set aside. Add up to 1 table-spoon more oil as needed and heat until oil just begins to smoke. Add remaining meatballs and brown on all sides. Remove any excess grease from wok and return first batch of meatballs. Pour soy sauce mixture over all and add 1/2 cup broth. Bring to a boil, cover and simmer for 30 to 45 minutes or until meat is cooked through. Add up to 1/4 cup more broth as needed if liquid is absorbed while cooking. (Dish may be made ahead, covered and refrigerated at this point. To reheat, bring meatballs to room temperature before simmering 10 minutes or until heated through.) Just before serving, place spinach on top of meatballs in wok, salt lightly and, with a spatula, gently move meatballs to top of spinach. Cover wok and steam for 2 to 3 minutes, or until spinach is tender. Remove to serving plate, discard star anise and serve at once.

Stir-Fry Ham with Green Vegetable *Serves 2 American style, 4 to 6 Chinese style*

1   cup cubed ham
1   pound fresh spinach, washed,
      dried and cut in half
1   green onion, minced
1   small clove garlic, smashed and
      minced
1   teaspoon cornstarch
2   teaspoons Chinese rice wine or
      dry sherry
2   teaspoons light soy sauce
½   teaspoon sugar
¾   cup chicken broth
     Peanut oil
     Salt

PREPARATION: On a platter, arrange prepared ham, spinach, green onion and garlic. Set aside. In a small bowl, combine cornstarch, wine, soy sauce, sugar and 3 tablespoons chicken broth. Set aside. Have additional chicken broth, peanut oil and salt ready to add as needed.

METHOD: Heat wok and add 1-1/2 tablespoons oil. Swirl oil with a spatula to coat sides of wok and heat until oil just begins to smoke. Add green onion and garlic, stir-frying until you detect the aroma. Add ham and stir-fry to heat through, about 1 minute. Add spinach and a pinch of salt. Stir-fry to combine. Pour 1/4 cup broth down sides of wok, cover and steam for 30 seconds. Remove cover, make a well and add cornstarch mixture. Stir-fry until the sauce clears. If serving this dish American style over rice, you will want more liquid; add 1/4 cup additional broth. Stir-fry to heat through. Remove to serving plate and serve at once.

Barbecued Pork *Makes 3 pounds*

A trip to Chinatown is not complete without the purchase of barbecued pork. Just pointing out the succulent pieces and watching as they are wrapped for take-out whets one's appetite. Here is a home-made version of this Chinese mainstay. Serve it as an appetizer or as an ingredient in other dishes.

3   pounds lean pork butt, cut into
      strips about 1½ by 4 inches
2   tablespoons hoisin sauce
¼   cup catsup
¼   cup sugar
2   tablespoons dark soy sauce
2   teaspoons Chinese rice wine or
      dry sherry
1   teaspoon Chinese hot oil (see
      page 49)
     Salt
     Water

PREPARATION: Cut pork into strips and set aside. In a bowl, combine hoisin sauce, catsup, sugar, soy sauce, wine and hot oil. Brush pork strips with sauce mixture and set aside for 3 to 4 hours at room temperature or overnight in the refrigerator. (Bring to room temperature before baking.) Line a roasting pan with aluminum foil and place baking rack in pan.

METHOD: Pour very hot tap water to a depth of 1 inch into roasting pan. Place pork on rack so slices do not touch one another. Bake at 375° for 45 minutes. Baste pork with any remaining sauce, turn pieces and bake for an additional 45 minutes. Remove from oven and sprinkle with salt. Allow to cool before serving or storing. Well wrapped, refrigerated barbecued pork will keep up to 1 week.

You have, no doubt, enjoyed crusty, deep-fried pork tidbits with sweet and sour sauce. Why not prepare this dish with baked pork. It's authentic, so much easier and just as tasty!

Easy Baked Sweet and Sour Pork   *Serves 3 to 4 American style, 6 to 8 Chinese style*

1½ pounds lean pork butt or pork steak, cut into 1 inch cubes
2 tablespoons light soy sauce
2 tablespoons Chinese rice wine or dry sherry
1 teaspoon salt
½ teaspoon sugar
1 can (8 oz.) pineapple, cut into bite-size pieces
1 cup Basic Sweet and Sour Sauce, unthickened
2 teaspoons cornstarch
1 large bell pepper, red or green, cut into 1 inch wedges
1 medium-size onion, cut into 1 inch wedges
2 tablespoons toasted, slivered almonds or peanuts

PREPARATION: In a bowl, combine pork cubes, soy sauce, wine, salt and sugar. Mix well and set aside for 30 to 45 minutes. Drain pineapple thoroughly in a colander. In a saucepan, combine sweet and sour sauce with 2 teaspoons cornstarch. Set aside. On a platter arrange drained pineapple, pepper, onion and nuts. Set aside. Line a baking sheet with aluminum foil.

METHOD: Spread pork pieces evenly on baking sheet and bake at 400° for 30 to 35 minutes, or until done. Do not overcook. Meanwhile, heat sweet and sour sauce over medium heat, stirring frequently, until sauce thickens and clears. Add pineapple, pepper and onion to sauce and simmer until vegetables are tender crisp. Place cooked meat in a serving dish and pour sauce over meat. Garnish with slivered nuts.

Basic Sweet and Sour Sauce   *Makes 2½ cups*

1 cup rice wine vinegar or white distilled vinegar
1 cup brown sugar, firmly packed
½ cup catsup
2 tablespoons light soy sauce
1 cup water
2 teaspoons Worcestershire sauce

In a saucepan over low heat, combine vinegar and brown sugar. Bring to a boil, reduce heat and simmer, stirring, until sugar is thoroughly dissolved. Stir in catsup, soy sauce, water and Worcestershire sauce. Simmer for 10 to 15 minutes. Remove from heat and cool slightly. Pour into a glass jar, seal tightly and refrigerate for up to 2 months.

To thicken sauce, stir or shake mixture and pour required amount into a saucepan. Stir in 1 teaspoon cornstarch per 1/2 cup sauce mixture. If garlic or ginger seasoning is desired, add 1/4 teaspoon garlic juice or ginger juice per 1 cup sauce. Over low heat, bring sauce to a simmer, stirring occasionally, until it clears and thickens.

A favorite Cantonese family dish uses barbecued pork with bok choy and tofu. By adding a little more liquid you can serve it over rice. It's a quick and easy way to fix a family supper in just minutes.

Stir-Fry Pork with Tofu and Bok Choy *Serves 3 to 4 American style, 6 to 8 Chinese style*

1   cup cubed Chinese barbecued
        pork (see page 64)
1   pound bok choy, stalks cut diag-
        onally in 1½ inch pieces, leafy
        portion cut into 1½ inch pieces
2   Chinese-style tofu cakes or
        canned tofu, pressed and cubed
1   green onion, minced
1   small clove garlic, smashed and
        minced
1   teaspoon cornstarch
2   teaspoons Chinese rice wine or
        dry sherry
1   teaspoon light soy sauce
½   teaspoon sugar
¾   cup chicken broth or water
    Salt
    Peanut oil

PREPARATION: On a large platter, arrange prepared pork, bok choy, tofu, green onion and garlic. Set aside. In a small bowl, combine cornstarch, wine, soy sauce, sugar and 3 tablespoons broth. Have additional broth, salt and oil ready to add as needed.

METHOD: Heat wok and add 2 tablespoons oil. With spatula, swirl oil around sides to coat wok and heat until oil just begins to smoke. Add green onion and garlic, stir-frying until you detect the aroma. Add tofu and stir-fry gently to combine. Add pork and stir-fry for 1 minute. Add bok choy, stir-fry briefly and add 1/4 cup broth. Cover and steam for 1 to 2 minutes, until vegetables are tender crisp. Remove cover, make a well and add cornstarch mixture. Stir-fry to combine and continue to cook until sauce clears. If serving this dish American style, over rice, you will want more liquid. Add additional broth; stir-fry to heat through. Remove to serving plate and serve at once.

Ginger Juice

Whip this up in minutes and have ginger ready to use any time. 1 teaspoon ginger juice will replace 1 slice ginger root in most recipes.

½   cup ginger root, sliced across the
        grain ¼ inch thick
1   cup light soy sauce
2   tablespoons Kaoliang wine,
        vodka or gin

In a blender or food processor, combine ginger and soy sauce. Process until ginger is puréed. Pour into a glass container with a tight-fitting lid and add liquor. Cover tightly and refrigerate. Before using, stir or shake well. Mixture will keep indefinitely.

Try this as a delicious entrée. Or serve these bite-size pieces as a memorable appetizer.

Red-Cooked Pork Ribs or Tidbits *Serves 3 to 4 American style, 6 to 8 Chinese style*

1½   pounds pork spareribs *or* 1 pound
        lean pork butt
1   clove garlic, smashed and minced
½   teaspoon five spice powder
2   tablespoons dark soy sauce
2   tablespoons Chinese rice wine or
        dry sherry
3   tablespoons brown sugar, firmly
        packed
2   tablespoons peanut oil
        Hot tap water

PREPARATION: If using pork ribs, have the butcher cut them into 1 to 1-1/2 inch pieces across the bone; trim off all excess fat. If using pork butt, trim fat and cut meat into 1 to 1-1/2 inch cubes. Set aside. Mince garlic and set aside. Measure five spice powder, soy sauce, wine and brown sugar to have ready to add as needed. Have oil and water at hand.

METHOD: In a heavy frying pan with a tight-fitting lid, heat oil until it begins to smoke. Add garlic and sauté until you detect the aroma. Add pork and sauté to brown lightly. Remove any excess oil with a bulb baster or spoon. Sprinkle pork with five spice powder and toss to combine. Add sugar, soy sauce and wine. Stir to combine and add *just enough* hot water to *barely* cover pork. Cover pan and bring to a boil. Reduce heat and simmer for 40 to 60 minutes, stirring occasionally. After 35 minutes, check pork to see if sauce is thickening and coating meat. If sauce does not appear thick enough, remove cover for the last minutes of cooking. To make this dish ahead of time, simmer for 35 minutes and refrigerate until ready to serve. Just before serving, reheat and allow to simmer for at least 10 minutes, or until sauce coats meat and dish is heated through. Remove to serving dish and serve at once.

Garlic Juice

With garlic juice, you have fresh garlic instantly, without peeling and mincing, for dishes of every description—from Stir-Fry Beef to Italian Lasagne. Use 1/2 teaspoon garlic juice in place of 1 clove garlic.

1   medium-size head garlic, about
        ¼ cup, each clove peeled
½   cup light soy sauce
1   tablespoon Kaoliang wine,
        vodka or gin

In a blender or food processor, combine peeled garlic and soy sauce. Process until garlic is puréed. Allow to rest a few moments until foam subsides. Pour mixture into a glass container with a tight-fitting lid and add liquor. Cover tightly and refrigerate. Before using, stir or shake well. Mixture will keep indefinitely.

One of the popular dishes served with Mandarin pancakes is Mu Shu Pork. Here is the summer version brimming with fresh bell peppers and bean sprouts.

Mu Shu Pork - Summer Recipe *Serves 3 to 4 American style, 6 to 8 Chinese style*

½ pound lean pork butt, sliced
1 teaspoon cornstarch
1 tablespoon light soy sauce
1 teaspoon Chinese rice wine or
  dry sherry
  Peanut oil
2 slices ginger root, smashed and
  minced
2 green bell peppers, shredded
½ pound bean sprouts, washed and
  drained thoroughly
4 soaked cloud ears (see page 27),
  broken into bite-size pieces
4 fresh mushrooms, sliced
1 egg
  Salt
  Water
2 green onions, shredded
  Hoisin sauce
8 Mandarin pancakes, see page 119,
  warmed

PREPARATION: In a small bowl, combine pork slices with cornstarch, soy sauce, wine and 1-1/2 teaspoons oil. Set aside for 15 to 20 minutes. On a platter arrange prepared ginger, green pepper, bean sprouts, cloud ears and mushrooms. Set aside. In a small bowl, beat egg lightly with a pinch of salt and 1-1/2 teaspoons water. Set aside. In separate bowls, have green onions and hoisin sauce ready to serve as garnishes. Have Mandarin pancakes, oil, salt and water at hand.

METHOD: Heat wok and add 1 tablespoon oil. With a spatula, swirl oil around to coat sides of wok and heat until oil just begins to smoke. Add egg and stir-fry quickly to scramble. Remove from wok and set aside. If necessary, wipe wok with a paper towel. To wok add 1 tablespoon oil and heat until oil just begins to smoke. Add green pepper, mushrooms and a pinch of salt. Stir-fry for 10 seconds and sprinkle 1 tablespoon water down sides of wok. Stir-fry until vegetables are tender crisp, about 1 to 2 minutes. Add cloud ears and stir-fry for 30 seconds to heat through. Remove from wok and set aside. To wok add 1-1/2 table-spoons oil and heat until oil just begins to smoke. Add ginger and stir-fry until golden brown. Add pork, spreading it in a single layer and stir-fry for 2 to 3 minutes. Add bean sprouts and stir-fry briefly to combine. Return vegetables and egg to wok, breaking egg into small pieces with a spatula. Stir-fry to combine. Remove to a serving plate. Serve at once with warmed Mandarin pancakes (see page 119), garnished with green onions and hoisin sauce.

To serve with Mandarin pancakes: Spread 1 teaspoon hoisin sauce down the center of each warmed pancake, add 2 to 3 tablespoons meat mixture, sprinkle with green onion, roll up pancake and eat out of hand.

Mu Shu Pork is a favorite all year long. In the winter, when fresh ingredients are not available, the Chinese substitute dried ingredients.

Mu Shu Pork - Winter Recipe *Serves 3 to 4 American style, 6 to 8 Chinese style*

½ pound lean pork butt, sliced
2 teaspoons cornstarch
3 teaspoons Chinese rice wine or
     dry sherry
2 tablespoons light soy sauce
    Peanut oil
¼ cup chicken broth or water
½ teaspoon sugar
1 tablespoon vinegar
4 soaked cloud ears (see page 27),
     broken into bite-size pieces
4 soaked dried black mushrooms
     (see page 28), sliced
10 soaked golden needles (see
     page 31), tied in knots
1 bamboo shoot, cut into match-
     stick-size pieces, about
     ½ cup
2 eggs
1 tablespoon water
    Salt
3 green onions, shredded
    Hoisin sauce
    Sesame oil
8 Mandarin Pancakes, see page
     119, warmed

PREPARATION: In a small bowl, combine sliced pork, 1 teaspoon cornstarch, 1 teaspoon wine, 1 tablespoon soy sauce and 1-1/2 teaspoons peanut oil. Set aside for 15 to 20 minutes. In a small bowl, combine 1 teaspoon cornstarch, chicken broth, 2 teaspoons wine, sugar, 1 tablespoon soy sauce and vinegar. Set aside. On a large platter arrange prepared cloud ears, mushrooms, golden needles and bamboo shoot. Set aside. In a small bowl, beat eggs lightly with 1 tablespoon water and a pinch of salt. Set aside. In separate bowls, have green onions and hoisin sauce ready to serve as garnishes. Have sesame oil, Mandarin pancakes, peanut oil, salt and water at hand.

METHOD: Heat wok and add 1-1/2 tablespoons peanut oil. With spatula, swirl oil around to coat sides of wok and heat until oil just begins to smoke. Add eggs and stir-fry quickly to scramble. Remove from wok and set aside. If necessary, wipe wok with a paper towel. In wok, heat 1 tablespoon peanut oil until oil begins to smoke. Add cloud ears, mushrooms, golden needles and bamboo shoot. Stir-fry briefly, add a pinch of salt and sprinkle 1 tablespoon water down sides of wok. Continue to stir-fry until vegetables are tender crisp, about 2 minutes. Remove from wok and set aside. In wok heat 2 tablespoons peanut oil until oil just begins to smoke. Add pork, spreading it in a single layer, and stir-fry for 2 to 3 minutes. Return vegetables to wok and stir-fry to combine. Make a well and add cornstarch mixture. Stir-fry until sauce thickens and clears. Return eggs to wok, breaking them into bite-size pieces with spatula. Stir-fry to combine and add sesame oil. Remove to serving platter and serve with warmed Mandarin pancakes, hoisin sauce and green onions.

To serve with Mandarin pancakes: Spread 1 teaspoon hoisin sauce down the center of each warmed pancake, add 2 to 3 tablespoons meat mixture, sprinkle with green onion, roll up pancake and eat out of hand.

Lamb was introduced to the Chinese by the Mongolians. Here it is in a savory stir-fry dish with plum sauce.

Stir-Fry Lamb with Plum Sauce *Serves 3 to 4 American style, 6 to 8 Chinese style*

1   pound lean lamb, cut from round bone or shoulder chop, shredded
2   teaspoons cornstarch
3   tablespoons light soy sauce
     Peanut oil
1   large onion, cut into eighths with the grain
3   cloves garlic, smashed and minced
3   slices ginger root, smashed and minced
2   tablespoons plum sauce
½   cup chicken broth or water (optional)
     Salt
     Water

PREPARATION: In a small bowl, combine shredded lamb, cornstarch, soy sauce and 1 tablespoon oil. Set aside for 15 to 20 minutes. On a platter, arrange prepared onion, garlic and ginger. Set aside. Have plum sauce and broth measured; have salt, oil and water at hand and ready to add as needed.

METHOD: Heat wok and add 1 tablespoon oil. With spatula, swirl oil to coat sides of wok and heat until oil just begins to smoke. Add onion, a pinch of salt and stir-fry for 30 seconds. Sprinkle 1 tablespoon water down sides of wok and continue to stir-fry until tender crisp, about 2 minutes. Remove from wok and set aside. To wok add 2-1/2 tablespoons oil and heat until oil just begins to smoke. Add garlic and ginger and stir-fry until golden brown. Add lamb, spreading it in a single layer, and stir-fry for 1 to 2 minutes. Return onions to wok and stir-fry to combine. Add plum sauce and stir-fry to combine. If serving this dish American style over rice you will want more liquid; make a well, add broth and stir-fry to heat through. Remove to a serving dish and serve at once.

Lamb in the Szechwan manner with dried red chiles and chili paste. Add the spicy chili paste sparingly as you can always add more to taste.

Stir-Fry Hot Spicy Lamb *Serves 3 to 4 American style, 6 to 8 Chinese style*

1   pound lean boneless lamb, sliced
3   tablespoons oyster sauce
2½ teaspoons cornstarch
    Peanut oil
3   cloves garlic, smashed and minced
3   slices ginger root, smashed and
      minced
4   dried red chile peppers, seeds
      removed
1   bunch green onions, cut into
      2 inch lengths
2   ribs celery, diagonally shredded
2   carrots, diagonally shredded
    Chili paste, 1 to 2 teaspoons
      (optional)
1   tablespoon red wine vinegar
    Salt
    Water

PREPARATION: In a small bowl, combine sliced lamb, oyster sauce, cornstarch and 1 tablespoon oil. Set aside for 15 to 20 minutes. On a large platter, arrange prepared garlic, ginger, chile peppers, green onions, celery, and carrots. Set aside. Measure out chili paste and vinegar to add as needed. Set aside. Have salt, oil and water at hand.

METHOD: Heat wok and add 1 tablespoon oil. With a spatula, swirl oil around to coat sides of wok and heat until oil just begins to smoke. Add celery, stir-fry 1 minute and add carrots. Stir-fry to combine, add a pinch of salt and sprinkle 1 tablespoon of water down sides of wok. Stir-fry for 1 minute. Add green onions; stir-fry until you detect the aroma of the onions. Remove vegetables from wok and set aside. To wok add 2-1/2 tablespoons oil and heat until oil just begins to smoke. Add chile peppers and stir-fry until they turn dark brown. Remove peppers from oil and discard. Add ginger and garlic to oil and stir-fry until golden brown. Add lamb, spreading it in a single layer, and stir-fry for 1 to 2 minutes. Return vegetables to wok, add vinegar and chili paste. Stir-fry to combine. If serving this dish American style over rice, you will want more liquid so make a well and add up to 1/2 cup additional water. Stir-fry until heated through; remove to a serving platter and serve at once.

Saté, an Indonesian dish adopted by the Chinese, features a unique peanut butter sauce. Serve it as an entrée or as a hot appetizer. It's bound to become a classic in your cooking repetoire.

Lamb or Pork Saté *Serves 3 to 4 American style, 4 to 6 Chinese style*

3 tablespoons peanut butter
1 tablespoon oyster sauce
2 tablespoons dark soy sauce
1 tablespoon red wine vinegar or cider vinegar
¼ cup Chinese rice wine or dry sherry
1 teaspoon sesame oil
2 teaspoons sugar
2 tablespoons peanut oil
2 cloves garlic, smashed and minced
2 slices ginger root, smashed and minced
2 dried red chile peppers, minced and seeds removed *or* 2 teaspoons Tabasco sauce
½ teaspoon salt
¼ teaspoon pepper
1 pound lamb or pork steak meat, cut into 1 inch cubes
Water

PREPARATION: In a bowl, combine peanut butter, oyster sauce, soy sauce, vinegar, wine, sesame oil, sugar, peanut oil, minced garlic, ginger and chile peppers, salt and pepper. Mix with a wire whisk to blend thoroughly. (If desired, sauce may be made ahead to this point and refrigerated in an airtight container for 3 to 4 days. Allow sauce to reach room temperature before proceeding.) Add lamb or pork cubes to sauce, stir to coat and set aside for up to 1 hour. Line a baking sheet with aluminum foil. Soak bamboo skewers in water for 5 minutes. Place meat on skewers, 4 to 5 pieces per skewer, leaving space between each piece. Place skewers on baking sheet. Set remaining sauce aside and reserve.

METHOD: Heat oven to 400° and bake saté for 10 minutes. Turn skewers and bake an additional 10 minutes. Remove from baking sheet and place on serving platter. Set aside and keep warm. In a small saucepan, bring remaining sauce and any drippings from the baking sheet to a boil with 1/2 cup water. Remove and serve in a sauce boat. Serve meat on skewers accompanied by rice.

This dish may be served as an appetizer. To serve, remove meat from skewers and serve with toothpicks.

A Feast of Chicken

Chicken has always been important in the Chinese diet. It is stir-fried, red-cooked, deep-fried, poached and steamed. It is served mildly seasoned or peppery hot, right off the fire or cold in a salad. There are, it is said, literally thousands of recipes for chicken in Chinese cuisine. Here is just a sampling of this glorious variety.

Baked Chicken Legs in Hoisin Sauce *Serves 3 to 4 American style, 6 to 8 Chinese style*

Here's a dish that bakes in the oven while you are busy stir-frying the rest of the meal. Serve it with a Chinese dinner or take it along on a summer picnic.

12 chicken drumsticks
    Peanut oil
½ cup light soy sauce
½ cup brown sugar, firmly packed
3 tablespoons hoisin sauce
1 clove garlic, smashed and minced
1 slice ginger root, smashed and minced
1 teaspoon Chinese rice wine or dry sherry
½ teaspoon salt

PREPARATION: Rinse and dry chicken legs. Set aside. Line a jelly roll pan with aluminum foil and brush foil lightly with peanut oil. In a small bowl, combine soy sauce, brown sugar, hoisin sauce, garlic, ginger, wine and salt. Set aside.

METHOD: Heat oven to 375°. Dip chicken legs in sauce mixture, draining off excess, and arrange on foil, leaving at least 1 inch between pieces. Bake for 30 minutes. Remove from oven, rotate chicken and brush with remaining sauce mixture. Return chicken to oven and bake 25 to 30 minutes or until done. Remove to a serving dish.

Chicken combines beautifully with green bell pepper, black mushrooms and nuts. Use the sweet bean paste, if you wish, for added sweetness.

Stir-Fry Chicken with Vegetables *Serves 3 to 4 American style, 4 to 6 Chinese style*

1   chicken breast (about 1 lb.), skinned, boned and cubed
1   teaspoon cornstarch
1   teaspoon light soy sauce
2   teaspoons Chinese rice wine or dry sherry
    Salt
    Peanut oil
1   green onion, minced
1   slice ginger root, smashed and minced
1   green bell pepper, cut into 1/2 inch pieces *or* 1/2 cup green peas, fresh or frozen
½   cup cubed bamboo shoots
4   water chestnuts, diced
5   soaked dried black mushrooms (see page 28), quartered *or* 1 (4 oz.) can mushrooms, well drained and liquid reserved
1   tablespoon hoisin sauce
½   teaspoon sweet bean paste (optional)
½   cup liquid reserved from mushrooms or broth
    Water
½   cup blanched cashews, almonds or peanuts, stir-fried (see page 77)

PREPARATION: In a small bowl, combine cubed chicken, cornstarch, soy sauce, wine, 1/2 teaspoon salt and 2 teaspoons oil. Set aside for 15 to 20 minutes. On a platter, arrange prepared green onion, ginger, green pepper, bamboo shoots, water chestnuts and mushrooms. Set aside. In a small bowl, combine hoisin sauce with sweet bean paste. Set aside. Have liquid reserved from mushrooms, salt, water, cashews and peanut oil ready to add as needed.

METHOD: Heat wok and add 2 tablespoons oil. With spatula, swirl oil to coat sides of wok and heat until oil just begins to smoke. Add green onion and ginger and stir-fry until you detect the aroma. Add chicken, spreading it in a single layer, and stir-fry for 2 to 3 minutes or until pink color is gone. Remove from wok and set aside. To wok add 1 tablespoon oil and heat until oil just begins to smoke. Add green pepper, stir-fry for 10 seconds, add a pinch of salt and sprinkle 1 tablespoon water down sides of wok. Stir-fry until tender crisp, about 2 to 3 minutes. Remove pepper from wok and set aside. To wok add 1 tablespoon oil and heat until oil just begins to smoke. Add hoisin sauce mixture and heat, stir-frying, until bubbling. Add mushrooms, water chestnuts and bamboo shoots. Stir-fry until heated through, about 1 to 2 minutes. Return chicken and green pepper to wok and stir-fry to combine. Make a well and gradually add liquid reserved from mushrooms. Stir-fry to combine. Remove to serving platter, garnish with cashews and serve at once.

You will find this dish listed as Kung Pao Chicken on Chinese restaurant menus. Named for a Chinese official who lived during the Ching Dynasty, this dish reflects the hot, fiery taste so popular in the Szechwan region.

Stir-Fry Chicken with Chile Peppers *Serves 2 to 3 American style, 4 to 6 Chinese style*

1 chicken breast (about 1 lb.), skinned, boned and cubed
2 teaspoons cornstarch
3 tablespoons light soy sauce
  Salt
½ egg white, lightly beaten
1 slice ginger root, smashed and minced
3 dried red chile peppers, seeds removed
1 green bell pepper, cut into 1 inch squares
1 small onion, cut into 1 inch squares
1 clove garlic, smashed and minced
1 green onion, minced
1 tablespoon Chinese rice wine or dry sherry
2 teaspoons sugar
1 teaspoon vinegar
3 tablespoons stir-fried peanuts (see page 77) or roasted peanuts
  Water
  Peanut oil

PREPARATION: In a small bowl, combine cubed chicken, 1 teaspoon cornstarch, 1 tablespoon soy sauce, 1/2 teaspoon salt, egg white and ginger. Set aside for 20 to 30 minutes. On a platter, arrange prepared chiles, green pepper, onion, garlic and green onion. Set aside. In a small bowl, combine 1 teaspoon cornstarch, wine, 2 tablespoons soy sauce, sugar and vinegar. Set aside. Have peanuts, salt, water and oil at hand.

METHOD: Heat wok and add 1 tablespoon oil. With a spatula, swirl oil around to coat sides of wok and heat until oil just begins to smoke. Add garlic and stir-fry until golden brown, about 30 seconds. Add green pepper and a pinch of salt; stir-fry for 1 minute. Add onion squares, another pinch of salt and sprinkle 1 tablespoon water down sides of wok. Continue to stir-fry until tender crisp, about 2 to 3 minutes. Remove from wok and set aside. To wok, add 3 tablespoons oil and heat until oil begins to smoke. Add dried chile peppers and stir-fry until they turn dark brown. Remove chiles from oil and discard. Add chicken to wok, spreading it in a single layer, and stir-fry until all pink color disappears, about 2 to 3 minutes. Return vegetables to wok and stir-fry to combine. Make a well and add wine mixture, stir-frying to combine. Remove to serving platter and garnish with peanuts and green onion. Serve at once.

This dish may be served with rice or in Mandarin pancakes, like Mu Shu Pork (see page 68).

Plum sauce adds a piquant, fruity flavor to this dish. It's an easy stir-fry favorite that's delicious with rice American style or as part of a festive Chinese dinner.

Stir-Fry Chicken in Plum Sauce   *Serves 2 to 3 American style, 4 to 5 Chinese style*

1	chicken breast (about 1 lb.), skinned, boned and shredded
1	teaspoon light soy sauce
1½	teaspoons cornstarch
2	teaspoons Chinese rice wine or dry sherry
½	teaspoon salt
	Peanut oil
2	large ribs celery, shredded diagonally
½	cup sliced water chestnuts
2	green onions, shredded
1	clove garlic, smashed and minced
7	soaked dried black mushrooms (see page 28), sliced
¼	cup plum sauce
½	cup reserved mushroom soaking liquid or water
	Few drops Tabasco sauce (optional)
	Salt
	Water

PREPARATION: In a small bowl, combine chicken pieces, soy sauce, cornstarch, wine, salt and 1-1/2 teaspoons peanut oil. Set aside. Arrange the celery, water chestnuts, green onions, garlic and mushrooms on a large platter. Set aside. In a small bowl, combine plum sauce with mushroom soaking liquid. Set aside. Have Tabasco, salt, water and oil ready to use as needed.

METHOD: Heat wok and add 1 tablespoon oil. With a spatula, swirl oil to coat sides of wok and heat until oil just begins to smoke. Add celery and stir-fry briefly; add a pinch of salt and sprinkle 1 tablespoon water down sides of wok. Stir-fry until tender crisp, about 2 to 3 minutes. Remove from wok and set aside. To wok add 1 tablespoon oil and heat until oil just begins to smoke. Add water chestnuts, stir-fry briefly, add mushrooms and green onions. Stir-fry until you detect the aroma of the onions. Remove vegetables from wok and set aside. Add 2 tablespoons oil to wok and heat until oil just begins to smoke. Add garlic and stir-fry until golden brown. Add chicken, spreading it in a single layer and stir-fry until pink color is gone, about 2 to 3 minutes. Return vegetables to wok and stir-fry to combine. Make a well and add plum sauce mixture. Allow to boil and stir-fry briefly. Add Tabasco sauce and stir-fry to combine. Remove to serving plate.

Note: Dish may be made ahead and kept warm up to 30 minutes if wrapped in foil and placed in a warm oven or on a warming tray.

Stir-Fry Chicken with Oyster Sauce *Serves 2 to 4 American style, 4 to 6 Chinese style*

1   chicken breast (about 1 lb.),
      skinned, boned and cubed
3½ teaspoons cornstarch
3   teaspoons light soy sauce
2   teaspoons Chinese rice wine or
      dry sherry
    Salt
    Peanut oil
½   cup cubed bamboo shoots
½   cup cubed celery
½   cup cubed green bell pepper
4   soaked dried black mushrooms
      (see page 28), quartered *or*
      ½ cup fresh mushrooms,
      quartered
¾   cup blanched almonds or
      cashews, stir-fried (see recipe)
1   teaspoon oyster sauce
½   teaspoon sugar
3   tablespoons liquid reserved from
      soaking mushrooms or chicken
      broth
    Water

PREPARATION: In a bowl combine cubed chicken, 2 teaspoons cornstarch, 2 teaspoons soy sauce, wine, 1/2 teaspoon salt and 2 teaspoons oil. Set aside for 15 to 20 minutes. On a platter arrange prepared bamboo shoots, celery, green pepper, and mushrooms. Set aside. Have stir-fried nuts ready to add. In a small bowl, mix together 1 teaspoon light soy sauce, oyster sauce, sugar, 1-1/2 teaspoons cornstarch and 3 tablespoons liquid reserved from soaking mushrooms. Set aside. Have oil, salt and water at hand.

METHOD: Heat wok and add 1 tablespoon oil. With a spatula, swirl oil around to coat sides of wok and heat until oil just begins to smoke. Add bamboo shoots, stir-fry briefly; add a pinch of salt and sprinkle 2 teaspoons water down sides of wok. Stir-fry for about 1 minute. Remove from wok and set aside. To wok add 1 tablespoon oil and heat until oil just begins to smoke. Add mushrooms and stir-fry briefly. Add a pinch of salt and sprinkle 2 teaspoons water down sides of wok; stir-fry for about 1 minute. Remove and set aside. Add 1 tablespoon oil to wok and heat until oil just begins to smoke. Add celery and green pepper. Stir-fry briefly. Add a pinch of salt and sprinkle 1 tablespoon water down sides. Stir-fry until vegetables are tender crisp, about 1 to 2 minutes. Remove from wok and set aside. Add 2 tablespoons oil to wok and heat until oil just begins to smoke. Add chicken, spreading it in a single layer, and stir-fry until pink color is gone, about 2 to 3 minutes. Return vegetables to wok and stir-fry to combine. Make a well and add oyster sauce mixture. Stir-fry until liquid clears and glazes the ingredients. Remove to a serving dish and garnish with prepared nuts. Serve at once.

To stir-fry almonds, cashews or peanuts, heat 1 cup peanut oil in wok to 375° or until a cube of bread dropped in oil rises to the surface and browns quickly. Add blanched nuts and stir-fry *just* until light brown. (Be sure to keep heat at an even temperature, since nuts burn easily.) Remove nuts at once and drain on paper towel; salt nuts lightly and set aside.

Velvet chicken is also known as smooth or slick chicken. Its lovely texture is obtained by coating the chicken meat with egg white and cornstarch before plunging it into seasoned boiling water. This method of cooking makes chicken especially tender and succulent. The chicken can be prepared ahead and refrigerated until needed in other recipes. Consult recipe to see whether chicken should be sliced, minced, shredded, cubed or diced.

Basic Velvet Chicken *Makes 2 cups*

Ice water
1½ pounds chicken breast, skinned, boned and cut according to recipe (about 2 cups)
1 egg white, slightly beaten
2 tablespoons cornstarch
2 quarts water
1 teaspoon light soy sauce
½ teaspoon salt

PREPARATION: Pour ice water into a large bowl and set aside. In a small bowl mix chicken with egg white and cornstarch. Set aside. In a saucepan, bring 2 quarts water, the soy sauce and salt to a boil. Have colander at hand.

METHOD: Add chicken to boiling water and stir gently to separate pieces. As soon as the water comes to a boil, remove pan from heat at once. Let chicken stand for 1 minute in hot water. Quickly drain in a colander and immediately plunge chicken into ice water. Remove and drain thoroughly. Use as directed in recipe or cover well and refrigerate until ready to use. Refrigerated velvet chicken will keep up to two days. (Bring to room temperature before using in recipe.)

One of the most popular chicken dishes calls for Velvet Chicken. The vegetables are stir-fried and then the chicken is steamed briefly. This is a dish the family will love.

Stir-Fry Velvet Chicken with Almonds *Serves 3 to 4 American style, 6 to 8 Chinese style*

2 cups diced Velvet Chicken (see preceding page)
1 teaspoon cornstarch
2 tablespoons chicken broth or water
1½ tablespoons light soy sauce
1 tablespoon oyster sauce
1 tablespoon Chinese rice wine or dry sherry
½ teaspoon sugar
½ cup green peas, fresh or frozen
1 clove garlic, smashed and minced
2 slices ginger root, smashed and minced
½ cup diced bamboo shoots
½ cup diced mushrooms, canned or fresh
4 water chestnuts, diced
¼ cup chicken broth or water
1 green onion minced *or* 1 tablespoon cilantro, minced
¼ cup blanched almonds, stir- fried (see page 77) or canned
Peanut oil
Sesame oil

PREPARATION: Have prepared velvet chicken at hand. In a small bowl, dissolve cornstarch in 2 tablespoons broth and add soy sauce, oyster sauce, wine and sugar. Set aside. If using fresh peas blanch them for 1 minute; if using frozen peas, defrost them. On a platter, arrange prepared peas, garlic, ginger, bamboo shoots, mushrooms and water chestnuts. Set aside. Have other ingredients ready to add as needed.

METHOD: Heat wok and add 2-1/2 tablespoons peanut oil. With spatula, swirl oil around to coat sides of wok and heat until oil just begins to smoke. Add ginger and garlic; stir-fry until golden brown. Add bamboo shoots, mushrooms and water chestnuts; stir-fry until heated through, about 1 to 2 minutes. Spread vegetables in a thin layer in wok. Add 1/4 cup broth and bring to a simmer. Lay velvet chicken on top of vegetables, cover and steam for 1 minute. Remove cover, add peas and stir fry to combine. Make a well and add soy sauce mixture. Stir-fry until all ingredients are glazed. Add a few drops of sesame oil and top with green onions or cilantro. Remove to a serving plate and garnish with almonds. Serve at once.

Mu Shu Chicken, as well as Mu Shu Pork, has always been considered a dish from North China. This delectable combination of meat, vegetables and mushrooms is scrambled with eggs and then wrapped in Mandarin pancakes and served with green onions and hoisin sauce.

Mu Shu Chicken   *Serves 3 to 4 American style, 6 to 8 Chinese style*

1   chicken breast (about 1 lb.), skinned, boned and shredded *or* a mixture of shredded breast and thigh meat, enough to make 1½ cups
2½   tablespoons light soy sauce
1   teaspoon cornstarch
1   teaspoon Chinese rice wine or dry sherry
  Peanut oil
2   slices ginger root, smashed and minced
½   cup shredded bamboo shoots
¾   cup shredded daikon radish (optional)
4   soaked dried black mushrooms (see page 28), sliced
4   soaked cloud ears (see page 27), broken into small bite-size pieces
3   eggs
  Water
  Salt
2   green onions, shredded
  Hoisin sauce
  Sesame oil
8.   Mandarin pancakes, warmed

PREPARATION: In a small bowl, combine shredded chicken, 1 tablespoon soy sauce, cornstarch, wine and 2 teaspoons peanut oil. Set aside for 15 to 20 minutes. On a platter, arrange prepared ginger, bamboo shoots, daikon radish, black mushrooms and cloud ears. Set aside. In a small bowl, lightly beat together eggs, 1 tablespoon water and a pinch of salt. Set aside. Place green onion and hoisin sauce in separate serving bowls and set aside. Have peanut oil, sesame oil, salt, soy sauce and water ready to add as needed. Have Mandarin pancakes at hand.

METHOD: Heat wok and add 2 tablespoons peanut oil. With a spatula, swirl oil around to coat sides of wok and heat until oil just begins to smoke. Add eggs and stir-fry quickly to scramble. Remove from wok and set aside. Wipe wok with a paper towel, if necessary. Add 2 tablespoons peanut oil to wok and heat until oil just begins to smoke. Add ginger and stir-fry until golden brown. Add chicken, spreading it in a single layer and stir-fry until pink color is gone, about 2 to 3 minutes. Remove from wok and set aside. Add 1 tablespoon peanut oil to wok and heat until oil just begins to smoke. Add vegetables from platter and stir-fry 10 seconds. Add a pinch of salt and sprinkle 1 tablespoon water down sides of wok. Stir-fry for 1 minute. Return chicken to wok and stir-fry to combine. Return eggs to wok, breaking them into small pieces with a spatula. Add 1-1/2 tablespoons soy sauce and a few drops sesame oil; stir-fry to combine. Remove to serving plate and serve with Mandarin pancakes, hoisin sauce and green onions (see page 68).

Another popular dish in Chinese restaurants is Egg Fu Yung. Serve it at home for a marvelous brunch or late supper. The whole family will love it.

Egg Fu Yung *Serves 2 to 3*

¾ cup chicken broth
2   teaspoons Chinese rice wine or
      dry sherry
1   tablespoon light soy sauce
1½ teaspoons cornstarch
1   teaspoon sesame oil
4   eggs
      Salt
1   cup shredded cooked chicken
¼ cup shredded bamboo shoots
½ cup bean sprouts, washed
      and drained
1   small onion, finely chopped
1   small slice ginger root, smashed
      and minced
      Pepper
      Peanut oil, for deep frying

PREPARATION: In a small saucepan, combine broth, wine, soy sauce and cornstarch. Heat, stirring constantly, until mixture clears and thickens, about 3 to 4 minutes. Remove from heat, add sesame oil and set aside. In a bowl, lightly beat eggs with a pinch of salt. Add prepared chicken, bamboo shoots, bean sprouts, onion, ginger and salt and pepper to taste. Set aside. Have 2 to 3 cups oil at hand.

METHOD: In a wok or other deep-frying pan, heat peanut oil to 350° or until a cube of bread dropped in oil rises to the surface and browns quickly. Carefully ladle about 1/4 egg mixture into oil and then another 1/4 amount. Cook each until the underside is golden brown, about 4 to 5 minutes. Turn and brown the other side, about 2 to 3 minutes. Remove from oil and drain on tempura rack or paper towels. Repeat with remaining egg mixture. Just before serving, reheat sauce, if necessary. Place Egg Fu Yung on warmed serving platter. Serve at once accompanied with sauce.

This dish is a perfect choice for a Chinese dinner along with a stir-fry dish or two. Use your wok to brown the chicken lightly and to combine the sauce. Then put it all in your oven to bake.

Red-Cooked Chicken with Onions *Serves 4 to 6 American style, 6 to 8 Chinese style*

Chicken drumsticks and thighs, about 7 of each
Pepper
½ teaspoon five spice powder
2 onions, sliced into thin rings
2 slices ginger root, smashed and minced
2 whole star anise
1 piece fresh orange peel, ¾ by 2 inches
⅓ cup dark soy sauce
⅓ cup water
2 teaspoons sugar
Peanut oil
⅓ cup Chinese rice wine or dry sherry

PREPARATION: With a heavy cleaver or very sharp, heavy knife, cut chicken legs in half across the bone. Cut thighs into 3 pieces, cutting off the heavy, meaty side and once across the bone. Place chicken on a large platter or baking sheet and sprinkle with pepper and five spice powder. Set aside. On a platter, arrange onion slices, minced ginger, star anise and orange peel. Set aside. In a small bowl, combine soy sauce and water. Set aside. Measure out sugar and have it ready to add as needed. Have oil and wine at hand.

METHOD: Heat wok and add 2 tablespoons oil. With a spatula, swirl oil around to coat sides of wok and heat until oil just begins to smoke. Add half of the prepared chicken and stir-fry until lightly browned, about 4 to 6 minutes. Remove chicken from wok and place in a 3 to 4 quart earthenware casserole with a lid. Cover and set aside. To wok, add 1 tablespoon oil and heat until oil just begins to smoke. Add remaining chicken and stir-fry to lightly brown. Add onions, ginger, star anise and orange peel. Stir-fry to combine. Sprinkle soy sauce mixture and sugar over all and stir-fry to combine. Remove to casserole. If your casserole lid does not have a steam hole, fold a piece of aluminum foil until it is about 1/2 inch thick and hook it over the side of the casserole to allow moisture to escape from under the lid during cooking. Place casserole in preheated 350° oven for 15 minutes. Reduce heat to 275° and bake for 1 hour, stirring casserole every 20 minutes. Remove casserole from oven, stir in wine, cover and continue to bake for an additional 45 minutes. Just before serving, remove orange peel and star anise. (This recipe may be made ahead and served chilled or at room temperature.)

Authentically, these drumsticks would be cooked over an open fire on a Genghis Khan grill. You can make them just as successfully in your oven.

Baked Chicken Legs with Garlic and Lemon *Serves 4 to 6 American style, 6 to 12 Chinese style*

12 chicken drumsticks
   Salt
   Pepper
   Juice of 1 lemon
   Grated lemon peel from ½ lemon
2 cloves garlic, smashed and minced
1 slice ginger root, smashed and
    minced
2 teaspoons light soy sauce
2 teaspoons sugar
2 tablespoons honey
½ teaspoon five spice powder
½ teaspoon paprika
½ cup flour
   Peanut oil

PREPARATION: Rub chicken legs with salt and pepper and set aside for at least 30 minutes. In a small bowl, combine lemon juice, lemon peel, garlic, ginger, soy sauce, sugar, honey and five spice powder. (If you wish, you may liquify these ingredients in a blender.) Set aside. Line a jelly roll pan with aluminum foil. In a small bag, combine paprika and flour. Pour a small amount of oil into a shallow bowl.

METHOD: Place chicken legs in bag, 3 or 4 at a time, and shake to coat with flour mixture. Brush each leg lightly with peanut oil and place on foil, making sure the legs do not touch. Bake for 30 minutes at 400°; remove from oven and brush legs on both sides with lemon mixture. Return chicken to oven and bake an additional 25 to 30 minutes, basting chicken 2 or 3 times. If chicken cooks too quickly, rotate pieces to prevent burning.

The Genghis Khan Grill

Here is a unique cast iron broiler you can use over the burner of your stove or outdoors over your barbecue. Set the grill over high heat and when it is sizzling hot, place the chicken legs (see recipe above) or thin slices of marinated meat over the dome. The juices will drain into the trough that encircles the grill. The Genghis Khan grill measures 10 inches in diameter. It can be purchased in oriental markets, import specialty stores and some gourmet stores.

In this recipe, the chicken is first quickly deep-fried and then added to the stir-fry vegetables. This Mandarin cooking technique adds a succulent difference.

Mandarin Chicken *Serves 2 to 3 American style, 4 to 6 Chinese style*

1   chicken breast (about 1 lb.), skinned, boned and cubed
Salt
2   teaspoons cornstarch
½   egg white, slightly beaten
½   cup diced bamboo shoots
½   cup quartered water chestnuts
½   cup quartered fresh mushrooms *or* 1 (4 oz.) can mushrooms, well drained
1   rib celery, sliced diagonally into ½ inch pieces
3   green onions, minced
2   teaspoons Chinese rice wine or dry sherry
¼   cup oyster sauce or soy sauce
½   cup chicken broth or water
½   teaspoon sugar
½   cup blanched almonds, stir-fried (see page 77)
Peanut oil
Water

PREPARATION: In a small bowl, combine cubed chicken, 1/2 teaspoon salt, 1 teaspoon cornstarch and egg white. Set aside for 15 to 20 minutes. On a platter, arrange prepared bamboo shoots, water chestnuts, mushrooms, celery and green onions. Set aside. Have wine measured and ready to add as needed. In a small bowl, combine oyster sauce, broth, 1 teaspoon cornstarch and sugar. Set aside. Have cooked almonds, peanut oil, water and salt ready to add as needed.

METHOD: In wok heat 1-1/2 cups oil to 375° or until a cube of bread dropped in oil rises to the surface and browns quickly. Add chicken and stir gently with spatula to separate pieces. Cook until all pink color is gone. Remove and drain chicken on paper towel. Set aside. Remove oil from wok and wipe wok with a paper towel. To wok add 1 tablespoon oil and heat until oil just begins to smoke. Add celery and a pinch of salt; stir-fry briefly. Sprinkle 1 tablespoon water down the sides of wok and stir-fry for 1 to 2 minutes. Add bamboo shoots and water chestnuts. Add a pinch of salt and stir-fry until vegetables are heated through. Remove from wok and set aside. To wok add 1 tablespoon oil and heat until oil just begins to smoke. Add mushrooms and a pinch of salt; sprinkle 1 tablespoon water down the sides of wok and stir-fry until mushrooms are heated through, about 30 seconds. Return cooked vegetables to wok and drizzle with wine. Stir-fry briefly and return chicken to wok, stir-frying to combine. Make a well and add oyster sauce mixture. Stir-fry to heat through. Add green onions and stir-fry to combine. Remove to a serving platter and garnish with almonds. Serve at once.

Traditionally, Lemon Chicken is made with a whole chicken chopped into bite-size pieces. This adaptation, using boned chicken thighs, will probably be more to your liking. The lemon seems to bring all the fresh flavors to a delicious peak.

Stir-Fry Lemon Chicken *Serves 4 to 5 American style, 6 to 8 Chinese style*

Chicken thighs, about 8 to 10, skinned, boned and cut into bite-size pieces
1½ teaspoons salt
½ teaspoon pepper
Peanut oil
5 soaked dried black mushrooms (see page 28), sliced *or* 6 fresh mushrooms, sliced
1 red or green bell pepper
5 green onions, shredded
3 slices ginger root, smashed and minced
Zest of 1 or 2 lemons (yellow part of peel only), slivered
½ cup liquid reserved from soaking mushrooms or chicken broth
2 tablespoons light soy sauce
1 teaspoon cornstarch
1½ teaspoons sugar
2 tablespoons Chinese rice wine or dry sherry
3 tablespoons lemon juice

PREPARATION: Rub chicken pieces with salt and pepper and place in a large bowl. Drizzle with 1 tablespoon peanut oil, toss lightly and set aside. On a platter arrange prepared mushrooms, pepper, onions, ginger root and lemon slivers. Set aside. In a bowl, combine liquid reserved from soaking mushrooms, soy sauce, cornstarch, sugar and wine. Have lemon juice and oil ready to add as needed.

METHOD: Heat wok and add 2 to 3 tablespoons oil. With a spatula, swirl oil to coat sides of wok and heat until oil just begins to smoke. Add chicken, spreading it in a single layer, and stir-fry until pink color disappears, about 2 to 3 minutes. Remove from wok and set aside. Add 1 tablespoon oil to wok and heat until oil just begins to smoke. Add ginger, mushrooms and pepper. Stir-fry for 1 minute. Add lemon slivers and green onion; sprinkle soy sauce mixture over all. Stir-fry to heat through. Return chicken to wok and stir-fry to combine. Drizzle lemon juice over all and stir-fry to heat through. Remove to a serving dish.

Note: Dish may be made ahead and kept warm for up to 30 minutes if wrapped in foil and kept in a warm oven or on a warming tray.

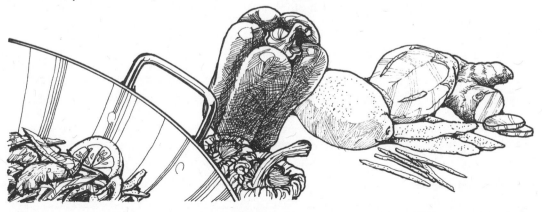

Fish and Seafood

The Chinese have always loved fish and are famous for their fish dishes. At a banquet, a beautifully prepared fish is served to signal the end of the main courses. At family dinners, fish is included on a daily basis. The delicious success of Chinese fish recipes depends upon the use of the freshest of fish and shellfish. (Often the fish is killed seconds before cooking.) Therefore when you are selecting seafood, be sure you buy the freshest available.

Sweet and Sour Fish *Serves 2 to 3 American style, 4 to 6 Chinese style*

The most famous Sweet and Sour Fish recipe originated in Hanan, a city south of Peking in the Northern region. Authentically a carp is used and is deep-fried, first over a hot and then over a slow fire. Here is a simpler version using cubed fish and a Basic Sweet and Sour Sauce.

1	pound halibut, ling cod, sea bass or red snapper, cut into 1 inch cubes
	Cornstarch
1	egg yolk
1	tablespoon all-purpose flour
1	teaspoon Chinese rice wine or dry sherry
	Salt
	Water
1	green onion, minced
½	cup Basic Sweet and Sour Sauce (see page 65), unthickened
2	cups peanut oil, for deep-frying

PREPARATION: Prepare fish pieces and dust them in 3 tablespoons cornstarch. Set aside. In a bowl, combine egg yolk, 1 teaspoon cornstarch, flour, wine, a pinch of salt and enough water to make a thin batter, about 1/4 to 1/2 cup. Set aside. Mince green onion and set aside. In a saucepan, combine sweet and sour sauce with 1 teaspoon cornstarch. Cook over medium heat, stirring occasionally, until sauce thickens and clears. Set aside. Have tempura rack or paper towel on hand; line a baking sheet with paper towels.

METHOD: In wok or other deep-frying pan, heat peanut oil until a cube of bread dropped in oil rises to the surface and browns quickly. With bamboo tongs, dip fish pieces into egg batter and place them carefully in hot oil. Do not overload wok; cook only 6 or 7 pieces at a time. Drain browned pieces on tempura rack or paper towel for a few minutes. Transfer them to lined baking sheet and place in warm oven. When all fish is cooked, remove to serving platter. Reheat sweet and sour sauce if necessary, and pour sauce over fish. Garnish with green onion and serve at once.

In this popular Chinese dish, the fish pieces are lightly coated with ground almonds and then deep-fried. It's guaranteed to become a family favorite.

Almond Crusted Fish   *Serves 2 to 3 American style, 4 to 6 Chinese style*

1   pound halibut, sea bass, mai mai, ling cod, rock cod or red snapper, cut into 1 to 1½ inch pieces
1   teaspoon cornstarch
1   teaspoon salt
1   teaspoon sugar
1   teaspoon Chinese rice wine or dry sherry
2   teaspoons ginger juice (see page 66) *or* 1 slice ginger root, smashed and very finely minced with 1 teaspoon light soy sauce
1   egg, slightly beaten
2   teaspoons light soy sauce
3   green onions, minced
1½ cups ground almonds *or* ¾ cup ground almonds and ¾ cup cornflake crumbs
    Peanut oil for deep frying, about 2 to 3 cups

PREPARATION: Cut fish into pieces and place in bowl. Set aside. In a small bowl, combine cornstarch, salt, sugar, wine and ginger juice. Pour this mixture over fish and set aside for 15 minutes. In a small bowl, beat egg lightly with soy sauce. Set aside. Mince onions and set aside. Place ground almonds on a piece of waxed paper. Have a wire rack handy. Line a baking sheet with paper towels.

METHOD: One at a time, dip fish pieces in egg mixture and coat lightly with almonds. Place on wire rack. Continue until all pieces are coated. In wok or other deep-frying pan, heat oil to 375° or until a cube of bread dropped into oil rises to the surface and browns quickly. With bamboo tongs, gently place fish pieces in hot oil, about 5 or 6 at a time. Do not overload wok; fish will brown quickly. Drain brown pieces on tempura rack or paper towels for a few minutes and transfer them to baking sheet. Place baking sheet in warm oven until all fish is prepared. Remove to serving dish and garnish with green onions. Serve at once.

Black mushrooms and cloud ears are used in this delicious stir-fry recipe.

Stir-Fry Fish with Vegetables *Serves 2 to 3 American style, 4 to 6 Chinese style*

1 pound halibut, ling cod or sea
    bass, cut into 1 inch cubes
Peanut oil
Salt
1 teaspoon light soy sauce
1 teaspoon cornstarch
¼ cup liquid reserved from soaking
    mushrooms (see below) or
    chicken broth
2 teaspoons Chinese rice wine or
    dry sherry
2 teaspoons oyster sauce
½ teaspoon sugar
6 soaked dried black mushrooms
    (see page 28), sliced
3 soaked cloud ears (see page 27),
    broken into bite-size pieces
4 green onions, chopped
4 slices ginger root, smashed and
    minced
½ pound broccoli stems, peeled
    and sliced diagonally or ½ cup
    green peas
Water

PREPARATION: In a bowl, combine fish pieces, 1 teaspoon oil, 1/4 teaspoon salt and soy sauce. Set aside. In a small bowl, mix together cornstarch with liquid reserved from mushrooms. Pour half of this mixture over fish. To remaining cornstarch mixture, add wine, oyster sauce and sugar. Set aside. On a platter, arrange prepared mushrooms, cloud ears, green onions, ginger and broccoli. Set aside. Have additional peanut oil, water and salt at hand.

METHOD: Heat wok and add 1/3 cup oil. With spatula, swirl oil to coat sides of wok and heat until oil just begins to smoke. Add fish and carefully stir-fry until almost done, about 2 to 3 minutes (do not overcook). Remove fish from wok and set aside. Wipe wok with paper towel. To wok add 2 tablespoons oil and heat until oil just begins to smoke. Add ginger and stir-fry until golden brown. Add broccoli, if used, and stir-fry for 10 seconds, add a pinch of salt and sprinkle 1 tablespoon water down sides of wok. Add peas, if used, black mushrooms, cloud ears and half of the green onions. Stir-fry until all vegetables are tender crisp, about 1 to 2 minutes. Return fish to wok and stir-fry gently. Make a well and add oyster sauce mixture. Gently stir-fry to combine. Remove to a serving platter and garnish with remaining green onion. Serve at once.

One of the easiest of fish dishes is Braised Fish Steaks. You will enjoy serving this recipe American style with rice, a vegetable and salad.

Braised Fish Steaks *Serves 2 to 3 American style, 4 to 6 Chinese style*

4	tablespoons cornstarch
1	pound fish steaks, halibut, sea bass, red snapper or mai mai, ¾ to 1 inch thick
1	green onion, minced
1	clove garlic, smashed and minced
1	slice ginger root, smashed and minced
3	soaked dried black mushrooms (see page 28), sliced *or* 3 fresh mushrooms, sliced
½	cup liquid reserved from soaking mushrooms or chicken broth
2	tablespoons light soy sauce
¼	cup Chinese rice wine or dry sherry
2	teaspoons sugar
½	teaspoon salt
	Peanut oil
2	tablespoons cilantro or parsley, minced
	Sesame oil (optional)

PREPARATION: Sprinkle cornstarch on a plate. Lightly dip fish steaks into cornstarch, shaking off excess, and place fish on a large platter along with prepared green onion, garlic, ginger and mushrooms. Set aside. In a small bowl, combine mushroom soaking liquid, soy sauce, wine, sugar and salt. Set aside. Have peanut oil, cilantro and sesame oil ready to add as needed.

METHOD: Heat a large frying pan which has a tight-fitting lid. Add 2 to 3 tablespoons peanut oil and heat until oil just begins to smoke. Add fish steaks and brown on both sides, about 5 to 7 minutes per side. Remove from pan and set aside. Add 1 tablespoon peanut oil to pan and add green onions, garlic and ginger. Sauté until you detect the aroma. Add mushrooms and wine mixture. Stir to combine. Return fish steaks to pan, cover and allow to simmer for 7 to 10 minutes, or until fish flakes when tested with a fork. Baste fish 2 or 3 times during cooking. If fish becomes too dry, add a little water. Remove fish to a serving plate; spoon basting sauce over fish and sprinkle with 3 or 4 drops sesame oil, if desired. Garnish with chopped cilantro and serve immediately.

The Chinese steam their cleaned fish whole but you may wish to remove the head and tail to make cooking a bit easier. The Black Bean Sauce gives a unique zest to this dish.

Steamed Fish with Black Bean Sauce   *Serves 2 American style, 4 Chinese style*

1   trout, flounder or sea bass (about 1½ lbs.), cleaned, rinsed and dried
1   tablespoon Black Bean Sauce (see recipe)
2   tablespoons light soy sauce
2   tablespoons hoisin sauce
3   slices ginger root, smashed and minced
4   green onions, minced
1   clove garlic, smashed and minced
¼   cup Chinese rice wine or dry sherry
2   teaspoons peanut oil
    Sesame oil

PREPARATION: Place fish on a platter and set aside. In a saucepan, combine mashed black bean sauce, soy sauce, hoisin sauce, ginger and green onions (reserving 1 to 2 tablespoons green onion for garnish). Remove 1 to 2 tablespoons of this sauce mixture to a small bowl and rub inside fish. Set fish aside. To sauce mixture in pan, add garlic and wine. Heat to boiling, remove from heat and set aside. Have peanut oil and sesame oil at hand.

METHOD: In a wok or other pan equipped for steaming, bring 2 to 3 cups water to a vigorous boil. Lower heat to medium. Place fish in a heatproof dish and place on steaming rack, steam plate or in bamboo steamer. Steam fish for 15 to 20 minutes, or until fish flakes easily when tested with a fork. Remove fish to a heated serving platter (remove skin if desired) and keep warm. Reheat sauce over low flame. In pipkin or very small saucepan, heat peanut oil until it smokes. Drizzle oil over fish; pour sauce over all. Garnish with reserved green onion and sesame oil. Serve at once.

Black Bean Sauce: Mash 1 tablespoon washed fermented beans with a mortar and pestle, or a fork, and combine with 1 clove smashed garlic. Stir-fry this mixture in wok for 1 to 2 minutes, or until you detect the aroma of the garlic. Sauce is now ready to be used in recipe.

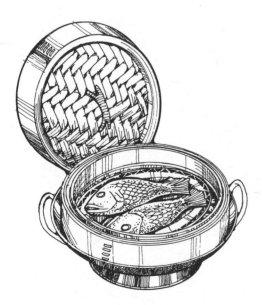

Shrimp is combined with mushrooms, peas and water chestnuts in this delicious, colorful stir-fry dish.

Stir-Fry Shrimp with Mushrooms and Peas *Serves 3 to 4 American style, 6 to 8 Chinese style*

1 pound medium-size shrimp, fresh
    or frozen, shelled, deveined
    and butterflied
    Lukewarm water
½ teaspoon baking soda
4 drops sesame oil
1 egg white, lightly beaten
1 teaspoon salt
1 tablespoon Chinese rice wine or
    dry sherry
2 teaspoons cornstarch
1 clove garlic, smashed and minced
1 slice ginger root, smashed and
    minced
¼ cup sliced water chestnuts
8 soaked dried black mushrooms
    (see page 28), halved *or* 1 (4 oz.)
    can button mushrooms, halved
1 cup green peas, fresh or frozen
¼ cup liquid reserved from
    mushrooms
    Peanut oil

PREPARATION: To butterfly shrimp, slit deveined shrimp down the front. Wash shrimp in a solution of lukewarm water and baking soda. Rinse well in cold water and dry on paper towels. Place shrimp in bowl, sprinkle with sesame oil and rub oil into shrimp. In a small bowl, combine egg white, salt, wine and cornstarch. Pour mixture over shrimp and refrigerate for 20 minutes. On a platter, arrange prepared garlic, ginger, water chestnuts, mushrooms and peas. Set aside. Measure out reserved liquid from mushrooms and set aside. Have peanut oil handy.

METHOD: Heat wok and add 2 tablespoons peanut oil. With spatula, swirl oil around to coat sides of wok and heat until oil just begins to smoke. Add garlic and ginger and stir-fry until golden brown. Add shrimp and stir-fry until tender (test with a fork), about 4 to 5 minutes. Remove from wok and set aside. Wipe wok with a paper towel. To wok add 1 tablespoon peanut oil and heat until oil just begins to smoke. Add water chestnuts, mushrooms and peas. Stir-fry to heat through, about 1 minute. Return shrimp to wok and stir-fry to combine. Make a well and add liquid reserved from mushrooms. Stir-fry to heat through, about 30 seconds. Remove to a serving plate and serve at once.

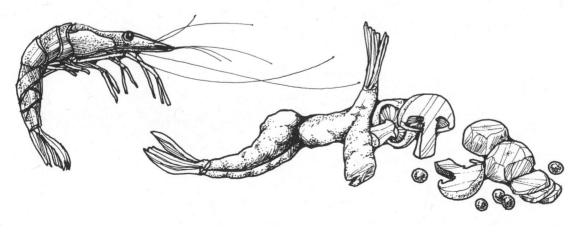

Hoisin sauce adds sweet-spicy flavoring to this remarkable shrimp dish. It's another dish you can serve American style over rice for a quick one-dish dinner.

Stir-Fry Shrimp in Hoisin Sauce   *Serves 3 to 4 American style, 6 to 8 Chinese style*

1   pound medium-size shrimp, fresh or frozen, shelled, deveined and slit down the back
     Lukewarm water
½   teaspoon baking soda
1   teaspoon cornstarch
     Peanut oil
1½   tablespoons hoisin sauce
1   tablespoon light soy sauce
3   tablespoons Chinese rice wine or dry sherry
1   cup green peas, fresh or frozen
1   clove garlic, smashed and minced
4   green onions, cut into 1½ inch lengths
2   slices ginger root, smashed and minced
     Water

PREPARATION: In a large bowl, wash prepared shrimp in a solution of lukewarm water and baking soda. Rinse in cold water and dry on paper towel. In a large bowl, combine prepared shrimp, cornstarch and 1 teaspoon oil. Set aside. In a small bowl, mix together hoisin sauce, soy sauce and wine. Set aside. If using fresh peas, blanch them 1 minute; if using frozen peas, defrost them. On a platter arrange prepared peas, garlic, green onions and ginger. Set aside. Have water and oil ready to add as needed.

METHOD: Heat wok and add 2-1/2 tablespoons oil. With spatula, swirl oil to coat sides of wok and heat until oil just begins to smoke. Add garlic and ginger and stir-fry until golden brown. Add shrimp and stir-fry about 2 minutes, until shrimp begins to turn pink. Add hoisin sauce mixture and stir-fry to combine. Add peas and green onions and stir-fry for 1 to 2 minutes. If serving this dish American style, over rice, add up to 1/4 cup water. Stir-fry to heat through. Remove to serving plate and serve at once.

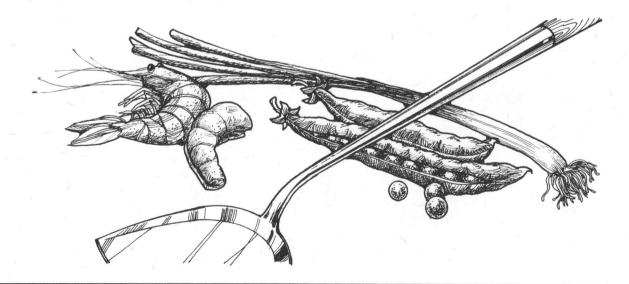

A nutritious combination of shrimp, tofu and spinach is prepared with spicy chili paste.

Stir-Fry Spicy Shrimp with Spinach and Tofu *Serves 2 to 3 American style, 4 to 6 Chinese style*

½ pound medium-size shrimp, fresh or frozen, shelled, deveined, and slit down the back
Lukewarm water
½ teaspoon baking soda
1 teaspoon Chinese rice wine or dry sherry
Peanut oil
Salt
2 teaspoons cornstarch
1 tablespoon light soy sauce
2 tablespoons chicken broth or water
1 teaspoon chili paste
1 (12 oz.) package Chinese-style tofu, pressed and cut into ¾ inch cubes
1 pound fresh spinach, stems removed, washed, dried and leaves cut in half
1 clove garlic, smashed and minced
½ cup chicken broth

PREPARATION: In a large bowl, wash prepared shrimp in lukewarm water and baking soda. Drain, rinse well in cold water and dry on paper towel. In a large mixing bowl, combine shrimp, wine, 1 tablespoon peanut oil and a pinch of salt. Set aside. In a small bowl, mix cornstarch, soy sauce, 2 tablespoons chicken broth and chili paste. Set aside. On a large platter, arrange prepared tofu, spinach and garlic. Set aside. Have chicken broth and additional peanut oil ready to add as needed.

METHOD: Heat wok and add 3 tablespoons oil. With a spatula, swirl oil around to coat sides of wok and heat until oil just begins to smoke. Add garlic and stir-fry until golden brown. Add tofu and stir-fry gently for 15 seconds. Add 1/2 teaspoon salt and 1/2 cup chicken broth. Lower heat and let simmer for 3 to 4 minutes. Add shrimp and stir-fry gently to combine. Cover wok and steam for 2 to 3 minutes, or until shrimp is pink and tender (test with a fork). Make a well and add cornstarch mixture. Stir-fry to combine. Add spinach, cover wok and allow to steam for 1 to 2 minutes. Remove to a serving plate and serve at once.

The Chinese have a way of bringing out the best in oysters. Try this stir-fry recipe and see for yourself.

Stir-Fry Oysters *Serves 3 to 4 American style, 4 to 6 Chinese style*

24 East Coast oysters, shucked, *or*
    2 (10 oz.) jars West Coast
    oysters
 2 slices ginger root, smashed and
    minced
½ cup sliced bamboo shoot
 2 green onions: 1 onion minced
    and 1 onion cut into 1 inch
    pieces
 2 cloves garlic, smashed and
    minced *or* 2 large shallots,
    minced
 1 teaspoon sugar
 3 tablespoons light soy sauce
 3 tablespoons Chinese rice wine or
    dry sherry
 1 teaspoon cornstarch
 1 tablespoon chicken broth or
    water
    Water
    Peanut oil

PREPARATION: If using fresh East Coast oysters, leave them whole. If using West Coast oysters, cut them in thirds. Set aside. On a platter, arrange prepared ginger, bamboo shoot, green onions and garlic. Set aside. In a small bowl, combine sugar, soy sauce and wine. Set aside. In another small bowl, mix together cornstarch and broth. Set aside. In a large bowl have 2 quarts cool water ready to use. Have oil at hand.

METHOD: In a saucepan, bring 1-1/2 quarts water to a boil. Add oysters, cooking East Coast oysters for 30 seconds and West Coast oysters for 45 seconds. Drain oysters and plunge immediately into cool water. Stir briefly and drain thoroughly. Set aside. Heat wok and add 2 tablespoons oil. With a spatula, swirl oil to coat sides of wok and heat until oil just begins to smoke. Add ginger, garlic and 1 inch green onion pieces. Stir-fry briefly, and add bamboo slices. Stir-fry for 1 minute. Add oysters and stir-fry 1 minute. Make a well and add soy sauce mixture. Stir-fry an additional 1 minute. Make a well and add cornstarch mixture. Stir-fry until mixture clears and makes a glaze, about 1 minute. Remove oysters to serving dish, garnish with minced green onion and serve at once.

The shallow-fry method is used in cooking these Oyster Fritters. Serve them as a part of your Chinese dinner or as an easy Sunday supper.

Oyster Fritters *Makes 6 to 8 fritters*

1½   cups oysters, fresh or canned, chopped into 1 inch pieces (reserve any liquid)
1   teaspoon Chinese rice wine or dry sherry
    Light soy sauce
4   eggs
5   tablespoons all-purpose flour
½   teaspoon baking powder
    Tabasco sauce
    Salt
    Pepper
5   green onions, minced
    Peanut oil
    Chinese hot oil (see page 49)

PREPARATION: In a bowl, combine chopped oysters, wine and 1 teaspoon soy sauce. Set aside. In a bowl, beat eggs and add flour, baking powder, and up to 1/4 cup reserved oyster liquid. Stir to combine and add Tabasco sauce, salt and pepper to taste. Add oysters and green onions. Heat oven to lowest setting and have baking sheet ready. Have peanut oil, Chinese hot oil and additional soy sauce at hand.

METHOD: Heat a large frying pan and add just enough peanut oil to coat bottom with a thin film. Drop oyster mixture by quarter cup amounts and brown fritters on one side, about 2 to 3 minutes. Turn fritters and brown the second side, about 1 to 2 minutes. As each fritter is cooked, place on baking sheet and keep warm in oven at lowest setting until all are cooked. Serve with hot oil and soy sauce, allowing each person to mix his own dipping sauce.

Vegetables - Tastier than Ever

The Chinese have a special way with vegetables. No matter how their vegetables are cut or cooked, they are always served tender crisp with all their natural color retained. Not only are the vegetables more appealing to the eye but they are also more nutritious as their vitamin and mineral content has not been cooked away.

Green Beans in Oyster Sauce *Serves 4 to 6*

1   pound green beans, washed, trimmed, cut into 1 inch pieces and blanched 3 minutes
1   medium-size onion, cut into eighths with the grain
4   fresh mushrooms, thinly sliced
2   tablespoons oyster sauce
1   tablespoon light soy sauce
2   tablespoons peanut oil

PREPARATION: Arrange prepared beans, onion pieces and sliced mushrooms on a platter. In a small bowl, combine oyster sauce and soy sauce. Set aside. Have oil ready to use as needed.

METHOD: Heat wok and add 1 tablespoon oil. With a spatula, swirl oil around sides of wok and heat until oil just begins to smoke. Add onion and stir-fry for 3 to 4 minutes. Add mushrooms and continue to stir-fry for 2 minutes. Remove vegetables from wok and set aside. In wok heat 1 tablespoon oil until it begins to smoke and add green beans. Stir-fry until tender crisp, about 4 to 5 minutes. Return onion and mushrooms to wok. Make a well and add oyster sauce mixture. Stir-fry to heat through. Remove to serving dish.

Dish may be covered with foil and kept warm for 15 to 20 minutes in a warm oven.

Here is a vegetarian dish that combines vegetables with protein-rich tofu.

Stir-Fry Spicy Vegetables with Tofu   *Serves 4 to 6*

2   medium-size carrots, diced and
      blanched 1 minute
1   cup green peas, fresh or frozen
5   soaked dried black mushrooms
      (see page 28), quartered *or*
      1 (4 oz.) can mushrooms,
      well drained and quartered,
      liquid reserved
½   cup diced bamboo shoots
2   cakes Chinese-style tofu,
      pressed and cut into ¾-inch
      cubes
1   clove garlic, smashed and minced
1   slice ginger root, smashed and
      minced
1   green onion, minced
2   dried red chile peppers, seeds
      removed
1   tablespoon hoisin sauce
1   tablespoon light soy sauce
1   tablespoon Chinese rice wine or
      dry sherry
¼   teaspoon sugar
1   teaspoon cornstarch
½   cup liquid reserved from
      soaked or canned mushrooms
    Sesame oil
    Peanut oil
    Water

PREPARATION: On a large platter, arrange prepared carrots, peas, mushrooms, bamboo shoots, tofu, garlic, ginger, green onion and chile peppers. Set aside. In a small bowl, combine hoisin sauce, soy sauce, wine and sugar. Set aside. In another small bowl, combine cornstarch with liquid reserved from mushrooms. Set aside. Have sesame oil, peanut oil and water ready to add as needed.

METHOD: Heat wok and add 2 tablespoons peanut oil. With a spatula, swirl oil to coat sides of wok and heat until oil just begins to smoke. Add carrots, stir-fry briefly and sprinkle 1 tablespoon water down sides of wok. Stir-fry for 1 minute. Add peas and stir-fry 1 minute. Add bamboo shoots and mushrooms; stir-fry to heat through. Remove vegetables from wok and set aside. To wok, add 2 tablespoons peanut oil and heat until oil just begins to smoke. Add chile peppers and stir-fry until they begin to darken. Remove from oil and discard. To oil in wok add ginger and garlic. Stir-fry until golden brown. Add tofu cubes and gently stir-fry until heated through. Add soy sauce mixture and cooked vegetables, stir-frying gently to combine. Make a well and add cornstarch mixture. Stir-fry to combine. Add a few drops sesame oil and remove to serving dish. Garnish with green onion and serve at once.

One of the easiest ways to cook vegetables is by steaming them. Be careful not to overcook them. The vegetables must be tender crisp. You will like them served the Chinese way—just drizzled with a simple hot dressing.

Chinese Style Steamed Vegetables

Vegetable, steamed tender crisp
1½   tablespoons peanut oil
1½   tablespoons oyster sauce, at
        room temperature

To serve, place drained, steamed vegetable on serving plate. In pipkin or other small saucepan heat peanut oil until sizzling. Drizzle oil and oyster sauce over vegetable. Serve at once.

Asparagus spears: Wash, trim and peel stem sections with a vegetable peeler. Arrange asparagus in 1 or 2 layers on steam plate, heatproof dish or bamboo steamer. Steam 6 to 8 minutes, or until tender crisp.

Sliced asparagus: Wash and trim asparagus and slice diagonally into 1/2 inch pieces. Place on steam plate, heatproof dish or bamboo steamer (layer should be no deeper than 3/4 inch). Steam 4 to 5 minutes, or until tender crisp.

Broccoli flowerettes: Cut flowerettes from main stalk, reserving stalk for other uses. Slice flowerettes into bite-size pieces. Drain well and arrange on steam plate, heatproof dish or bamboo steamer (layer should be no deeper than 3/4 inch). Steam 7 to 8 minutes, or until tender crisp.

Carrots: Wash and peel carrots. Cut into matchstick-size pieces or diagonally into 1/4 inch slices. Arrange on steam plate, in heatproof dish or bamboo steamer (layer should be no deeper than 3/4 inch). Steam 10 to 12 minutes, or until tender crisp.

Fresh peas: Remove from pods, rinse in cold water and drain well. Place on steam plate, heatproof dish or bamboo steamer (layer should be no deeper than 3/4 inch). Steam 5 to 6 minutes, or until tender crisp.

Zucchini (or Italian) squash: Wash and trim ends but do not peel zucchini. Slice diagonally in 1/2 inch slices and arrange in one or two layers on steam plate, heatproof dish or bamboo steamer. Steam 5 to 6 minutes, or until tender crisp.

Spinach: Wash spinach thoroughly, dry and cut in half. Place on oiled steam plate, heatproof dish or bamboo steamer. Steam 2 to 3 minutes, or until tender.

Cabbage: Shred cabbage and arrange on oiled steam plate, heatproof dish or bamboo steamer (layer should be no deeper than 1 inch). Steam 3 to 4 minutes or until tender.

Celery (or Napa) cabbage: Remove core and cut cabbage head lengthwise into quarters or sixths. Place pieces on oiled steam plate, heatproof dish or in bamboo steamer. Steam 3 to 4 minutes, or until tender.

Broccoli with Spicy Sauce *Serves 4 to 6*

Broccoli is given the Szechwan treatment when it is stir-fried with chili paste. Serve this at your next outdoor barbecue. Just use your wok over the barbecue grill.

1 large bunch broccoli (about
   1½ lbs.)
3 tablespoons water
1 tablespoon chili paste
1 tablespoon light soy sauce
2 tablespoons Chinese rice wine or
   dry sherry
1 tablespoon vinegar
2 tablespoons cooked ham, minced
   Peanut oil
   Salt

PREPARATION: Wash broccoli and separate stems from flowerettes. Peel stems and slice diagonally in 1/4 inch slices. Set aside. Cut broccoli flowerettes into bite-size pieces and set aside separately. Measure water into a cup and set aside. In a small bowl, combine chili paste, soy sauce, wine and vinegar. Set aside. Mince ham and set aside. Have oil and salt ready to add as needed.

METHOD: Heat wok and add oil. With a spatula, swirl oil around to coat sides of wok and heat until oil begins to smoke. Add broccoli stems and stir-fry for 10 seconds. Sprinkle lightly with salt and stir-fry for 1 minute. Add broccoli flowerettes and continue to stir-fry for 1 minute. Pour 2 tablespoons water down sides of wok, cover and steam for 2 minutes. Remove cover and test vegetables. If not tender crisp, add an additional tablespoon water and steam a bit longer. Remove cover, make a well and add chili paste mixture. Stir-fry until heated through, about 30 seconds. Remove to a serving dish, garnish with minced ham and serve at once.

Broccoli, carrots, baby corn and mushrooms are combined in a beautiful stir-fry dish. And it tastes just as good as it looks!

Colorful Stir-Fry Vegetables *Serves 4 to 6*

1 pound broccoli, peel stems and slice diagonally in ½ inch pieces, cut flowerettes into bite-size pieces

2 carrots, cut diagonally into ½ inch pieces and blanched 1 minute

1 cup canned baby corn (miniature ears), cut in half lengthwise

1 (4 oz.) can mushrooms, drained, sliced and liquid reserved

1 clove garlic, smashed and minced

1 slice ginger root, smashed and minced

1 tablespoon light soy sauce

1 tablespoon oyster sauce

   Chinese hot oil or Tabasco sauce

1 teaspoon cornstarch

1 tablespoon liquid reserved from canned mushrooms

   Salt

   Water

   Peanut oil

   Sesame oil (optional)

PREPARATION: On a large platter, arrange prepared broccoli, carrots, baby corn, mushrooms, garlic and ginger. Set aside. In a small bowl, combine soy sauce, oyster sauce and a few drops hot oil. Set aside. In a small bowl, combine cornstarch and liquid from mushrooms. Have salt, water, peanut oil and sesame oil ready to add as needed.

METHOD: Heat wok and add 1 tablespoon peanut oil. With spatula, swirl oil around to coat sides of wok and heat until oil just begins to smoke. Add garlic and ginger; stir-fry until golden brown. Add broccoli and a pinch of salt. Stir-fry to combine. Sprinkle 1 tablespoon water down sides of wok and cover to steam for 1 minute. Remove from wok and set aside. To wok add 1 tablespoon peanut oil and heat until oil just begins to smoke. Add carrots, stir-fry briefly and sprinkle 1 tablespoon water down sides. Stir-fry until tender crisp, about 2 to 3 minutes. Remove from wok and set aside. To wok add 1 tablespoon peanut oil and heat until oil just begins to smoke. Add baby corn and stir-fry briefly. Add mushrooms and stir-fry to heat through, about 1 to 2 minutes. Return broccoli and carrots to wok. Make a well, and add soy sauce mixture. Stir-fry to combine. Make another well and add cornstarch mixture. Stir-fry until sauce thickens and clears. Add a few drops of sesame oil. Remove to serving plate and serve at once.

Rice, Noodles and More

Like people everywhere, the Chinese depend on a starch in their diet. In the southern region, rice paddies abound and rice appears at every meal. In the morning, rice cooked as a gruel, called congee, is eaten. Rice fried with bits of meat, fish or vegetable is served at noon. At night, steamed rice accompanies dinner. Because rice absorbs any flavor and because its whiteness complements other ingredients, rice combinations are unlimited.

In the North, where wheat is grown rather than rice, the Chinese eat noodles and dumplings as their staple starch. Noodles are made in a variety of widths from ribbons to delicate strings. The dumplings consist of meat, fish or vegetable minced and enclosed in a wheat flour wrapper. Another renown wheat favorite is the Mandarin pancake, which is made to hold crispy pieces of Peking Duck or Mu Shu fillings.

Of course, all regions of China share in the enjoyment of rice and wheat as well as barley, millet, buckwheat and corn, but historically rice has predominated in the South and wheat in the North.

Always Perfect Steamed Rice *Makes 6 cups cooked rice*

2   cups long grain rice
    Cold water

Place rice in a heavy 1-1/2 quart saucepan which has a tight-fitting lid. To wash rice, fill pan with cold water and briskly rub rice between your hands. Drain off water and repeat washing until water runs clear. Drain off all water. Add 3 cups cold water and place pan over high heat. Bring to a boil, reduce to medium heat (do not cover); let rice boil until water evaporates and steam vents appear on the surface of the rice. Reduce heat to very low, cover and cook for 14 minutes. Turn off heat and allow to stand for 10 to 15 minutes. Just before serving, gently fluff rice. (To double recipe use 4 cups rice and 4-1/2 cups water.)

You can make more rice than needed for a meal and so have some cold rice on hand for fried rice and other recipes. Wrapped in aluminum foil, cooked rice will keep refrigerated for 10 days. Use cold rice as directed in recipe or reheat rice to serve plain. (Add 1 tablespoon water per cup of cooked rice when reheating.)

Leftover steamed rice is not a problem for the Chinese. They fry it the next day with whatever other leftovers they have on hand. Thus fried rice is always a "family". dish. However, you will find the following fried rice combinations so attractive and so delicious you'll want to serve them for company. For example, serve roast beef with fried rice instead of the usual potatoes.

Fried Rice with Ham and Shredded Lettuce *Serves 3 to 4 American style, 4 to 6 Chinese style*

2   eggs, lightly beaten
     Salt
½   cup shredded ham
2   cups shredded head lettuce
2   green onions, shredded
4   cups cold cooked rice
2   tablespoons light soy sauce
     Peanut oil

PREPARATION: In a small bowl, beat eggs lightly with a pinch of salt. Set aside. On a platter, arrange shredded ham, lettuce and green onions; set aside. Have rice and soy sauce measured; have oil at hand.

METHOD: Heat wok and add 1 tablespoon oil. With a spatula, swirl oil around to coat sides of wok and heat until oil just begins to smoke. Add beaten eggs and stir-fry to scramble. Remove from wok and set aside. If necessary, wipe wok with a paper towel. To wok add 2 teaspoons oil and heat until oil just begins to smoke. Add ham and stir-fry to heat through, about 1 minute. Remove from wok and set aside. To wok add 2-1/2 tablespoons oil and heat until oil just begins to smoke. Add rice and quickly stir-fry until very hot and steaming, about 5 to 7 minutes. Return eggs to wok, breaking them into bite-size pieces with a spatula. Add ham and stir-fry to combine. Add lettuce, green onions and soy sauce. Continue to stir-fry until well heated and thoroughly combined. Remove to serving dish and serve at once.

The Electric Rice Cooker

Perhaps you would like the convenience of an electric rice cooker. Made of stainless steel and aluminum, these rice cookers can prepare up to 15 cups of cooked rice at a time. The heating element maintains the proper temperature and, when rice is done, the cooker shuts off automatically. The result: moist, perfectly cooked rice every time.

Curried Fried Rice with Raisins *Serves 3 to 4 American style, 4 to 6 Chinese style*

½ cup raisins
   Warm water
½ cup green peas, fresh or frozen
½ cup red or green bell pepper,
   sliced into long thin strips
⅓ cup pine nuts or almond slivers
3 cups cold cooked rice
1 teaspoon curry powder
   Salt
   Water
   Butter, 2 to 3 tablespoons
   Peanut oil, 2 to 3 tablespoons

PREPARATION: In a small bowl, soak raisins in warm water for 30 minutes. Drain raisins thoroughly and place on platter. On the same platter, arrange peas, prepared pepper and nuts. Set aside. Have all other ingredients at hand and ready to add as needed.

METHOD: Heat wok and add 1 teaspoon butter and 1 teaspoon oil. Heat until butter sizzles. Add nuts and stir-fry briefly, until lightly browned and heated through. Remove nuts from wok, drain on paper towel and salt lightly. Set aside. To wok add 1 teaspoon butter and 1 teaspoon oil and heat until butter sizzles. Add pepper, a pinch of salt and sprinkle 1 tablespoon water down sides of wok. Stir-fry for 1 minute and add peas. Continue to stir-fry for 2 minutes or until vegetables are tender crisp. Remove from wok and set aside. To wok add 1/2 teaspoon butter and 1/2 teaspoon oil and heat until butter sizzles. Add raisins and stir-fry to heat through, about 1 minute. Remove from wok and set aside. Add 4 teaspoons butter and 4 teaspoons oil and heat until butter begins to sizzle. Add curry powder, stir-fry briefly and add rice. Stir-fry quickly until rice is heated through and begins to steam. Add 1-1/2 teaspoons salt, nuts, raisins and cooked vegetables; stir-fry to combine thoroughly. Remove to serving platter.

This dish may be made ahead and kept warm for up to 1 hour if covered with foil and placed on a warming tray or in a warm oven.

Five Precious Rice *Serves 3 to 4 American style, 4 to 6 Chinese style*

2   eggs
    Salt
1   chicken breast (about ½ lb.),
        skinned, boned and shredded
½   cup shredded ham
½   cup shredded bamboo shoots
½   cup sliced water chestnuts
2   green onions, minced
4   cups cold cooked rice
2   tablespoons light soy sauce
1   tablespoon Chinese rice wine or
        dry sherry
    Peanut oil

PREPARATION: In a small bowl, beat eggs lightly with a pinch of salt; set aside. On a platter, arrange prepared chicken, ham, bamboo shoots, water chestnuts and green onions. Set aside. Have rice measured and ready to add as needed. In a small bowl, combine soy sauce and wine. Set aside. Have oil and salt at hand.

METHOD: Heat wok and add 1 tablespoon oil. With a spatula, swirl oil around to coat sides of wok and heat until oil just begins to smoke. Add eggs and stir-fry quickly to scramble. Remove from wok and set aside. Wipe wok with paper towel, if necessary. To wok add 1 tablespoon oil and heat until oil just begins to smoke. Add chicken, spreading it out in a single layer, and stir-fry until pink color is gone. Remove from wok and set aside. To wok add 1 tablespoon oil and heat until oil just begins to smoke. Add ham and stir-fry 30 seconds. Add bamboo shoots and water chestnuts; continue to stir-fry until heated through, about 1 minute. Remove from wok; set aside. To wok add 2 tablespoons oil and heat until oil just begins to smoke. Add rice and stir-fry until rice is very hot and steaming, about 5 to 7 minutes. Return all cooked ingredients to wok, breaking eggs into bite-size pieces with spatula. Stir-fry to combine. Add green onions and soy sauce mixture. Salt to taste and stir-fry to combine. Remove to serving dish.

This dish can be made ahead and kept warm for up to 1 hour before serving if covered with aluminum foil and set on warming tray or in a warm oven.

Fried Rice with Beef and Vegetables   *Serves 3 to 4 American style, 4 to 6 Chinese style*

½   pound lean beef, sliced
2   teaspoons cornstarch
1   tablespoon light soy sauce
1   tablespoon Chinese rice wine or
      dry sherry
½   teaspoon sugar
      Peanut oil
1   medium-size onion, cut into
      eighths with the grain
1   green bell pepper, shredded
½   cup mushrooms, fresh or canned,
      sliced
2   green onions, minced
2   eggs
      Salt
4   cups cold cooked rice
2   tablespoons oyster sauce or light
      soy sauce
      Water

PREPARATION: In a bowl, combine beef slices, cornstarch, soy sauce, wine, sugar and 2 teaspoons oil. Set aside for 15 to 20 minutes. On a platter, arrange prepared onion, green pepper, mushrooms and green onions. Set aside. In a bowl, beat eggs lightly with a pinch of salt. Set aside. Have rice, oyster sauce, salt, water and oil at hand.

METHOD: Heat wok and add 1 tablespoon oil. With a spatula, swirl oil to coat sides of wok and heat until oil just begins to smoke. Add eggs stir-frying quickly to scramble. Remove from wok and set aside. Wipe wok with a paper towel, if necessary. To wok add 1 tablespoon oil and heat until oil just begins to smoke. Add onion pieces and green pepper; stir-fry 10 seconds, add a pinch of salt and sprinkle 1 tablespoon water down sides of wok. Stir-fry for 2 to 3 minutes, or until tender crisp. Remove from wok and set aside. Add 1 tablespoon oil to wok and heat until oil just begins to smoke. Add mushrooms and stir-fry briefly. Sprinkle 1 tablespoon water down sides of wok and stir-fry until mushrooms are tender, about 1 to 2 minutes. Remove from wok and set aside. Add 1-1/2 tablespoons oil to wok and heat until oil just begins to smoke. Add beef, spreading it in a single layer, and stir-fry for 2 to 3 minutes. Remove from wok and set aside. Add 2 tablespoons oil to wok and heat until oil just begins to smoke. Add rice and stir-fry quickly, until rice is heated through and begins to steam, about 5 to 7 minutes. Return all cooked ingredients to wok, breaking eggs into bite-size pieces with a spatula. Stir-fry to combine. Make a well, add oyster sauce and 1 teaspoon salt. Stir-fry to combine thoroughly. Remove rice to serving dish and garnish with green onions.

This dish may be made ahead and kept warm for up to 1 hour if covered with aluminum foil and placed on a warming tray or in a warm oven.

Fried Rice with Ham and Mushrooms   *Serves 3 to 4 American style, 4 to 6 Chinese style*

2 eggs
  Salt
½ cup green peas, fresh or frozen
½ cup cubed ham
1 (4 oz.) can mushrooms, well
    drained and chopped
2 green onions, minced
4 cups cold cooked rice
2 tablespoons light soy sauce
    (optional)
  Peanut oil

PREPARATION: In a small bowl, beat eggs lightly with a pinch of salt. Set aside. If using fresh peas, blanch them 1 minute; if using frozen peas, defrost them. On a platter, arrange prepared peas, ham, mushrooms, and green onions. Set aside. Have rice, soy sauce, salt and oil ready to add as needed.

METHOD: Heat wok and add 1 tablespoon oil. With spatula, swirl oil to coat sides of wok and heat until oil just begins to smoke. Add eggs, stir-frying quickly to scramble. Remove from wok and set aside. Wipe wok with a paper towel, if necessary. To wok add 1 tablespoon oil and heat until oil just begins to smoke. Add ham and peas, stir-frying until heated through, about 1 minute. Remove from wok and set aside. To wok add 1 tablespoon oil and heat until oil just begins to smoke. Add mushrooms and stir-fry until heated through, about 1 minute. Remove from wok and set aside. To wok add 2 tablespoons oil and heat until oil just begins to smoke. Add rice and stir-fry quickly, until rice is hot and steaming, about 5 to 7 minutes. Return all cooked ingredients to wok, breaking up eggs into bite-size pieces with spatula. Add salt to taste, and soy sauce. Add green onions and stir-fry to combine. Remove to serving platter.

This dish can be made ahead and kept warm for up to 1 hour if covered with aluminum foil and placed on warming tray or in a warm oven.

Clay Pot Cookers

The clay pot is the original stove-to-table server. Made of earthenware, this unique pot can be set right on the burner of your stove while the food cooks and then brought to the table. Clay pots come in many sizes, but a 1-1/2 quart size seems perfect for most families. You can purchase these clay pots in oriental markets and import specialty shops.

Chinese clay pot "casseroles" may not be as well known as wok dishes, but they are truly delicious. You can substitute any heavy pot for making these top-of-the-stove casseroles.

Clay Pot Rice with Clams, Shrimp and Peas *Serves 3 to 4*

1   cup uncooked long grain rice
     Cold water
1   (6½ oz.) can minced clams,
        undrained
¼   pound baby shrimp, shelled
        and cooked
1   tablespoon light soy sauce
2   teaspoons Chinese rice wine or
        dry sherry
1   small clove garlic, smashed and
        minced
1   cup green peas, fresh or frozen
1   green onion, minced
1   teaspoon sesame oil

In a Chinese clay pot, cover rice in cold water. Rub rice briskly between your hands until water is milky white. Drain and repeat washing until water runs clear. Drain thoroughly. To rice add undrained clams, shrimp, soy sauce, wine and garlic. Cover with 3/4 inch cold water. Cover pot and bring to a boil over high heat. Lower heat to simmer and cook for 12 minutes. Add peas and fluff rice. Cover and simmer an additional 12 minutes. Remove to a serving dish, garnish with green onion and sesame oil. Fluff rice and serve at once.

Steamed Chinese Sausages with Rice *Serves 2 to 3*

1   cup uncooked long grain rice
     Cold water
3   Chinese sausages, rinsed in
        warm water
2   green onions, minced
     Soy sauce
     Chinese hot mustard (see recipe
        page 43)

Use a Chinese clay pot or saucepan large enough to lay all sausages across the bottom and which has a tight-fitting lid. Put rice in pot and fill with cold water. Rub rice with your hands until water is milky white. Pour off water and repeat washing until water runs clear. Drain off all water, add 1-1/2 cups cold water and bring to a vigorous boil over high heat. Lower heat, cover and cook 1 to 2 minutes. Remove lid and place sausages in pot, pressing them into the rice. Replace lid and cook 5 minutes. Lower heat to a simmer and continue to cook 15 minutes. When rice is done, remove sausages and set aside. Fluff rice with a chopstick or fork, add half of the minced onion and stir to combine. Place in a serving dish. Slice sausages diagonally into 1-inch pieces and place on top of rice. Garnish with remaining green onion and drizzle lightly with soy sauce. Serve with soy sauce and Chinese hot mustard. (This recipe can be doubled to serve 4 to 6.)

Introduce the family and friends to rice sticks. In this delicious dish, they are served soft combined with shrimp and spinach and delicately flavored.

Stir-Fry Shrimp with Rice Sticks *Serves 2*

¼   pound rice sticks, broken in half
    Cold water
¾   pound medium-size shrimp, fresh
    or frozen, shelled and deveined
    Salt
1   tablespoon Chinese rice wine or
    dry sherry
1½ cups shredded spinach or celery
    cabbage
2   cloves garlic, smashed and minced
2   slices ginger root, smashed and
    minced
2   green onions, minced
1½ tablespoons light soy sauce
¼   cup chicken broth
    Chinese hot oil or sesame oil
    Peanut oil

PREPARATION: Soak rice sticks in cold water for 5 to 10 minutes. Drain thoroughly and set aside. Wash prepared shrimp in cold, salted water; drain and dry on paper towels. Cut shrimp in half crosswise. In a bowl, combine shrimp and wine and set aside for 10 to 15 minutes. On a platter, arrange spinach, garlic, ginger and green onions. Have all other ingredients at hand and ready to add as needed.

METHOD: Heat wok and add 2 tablespoons peanut oil. With a spatula, swirl oil to coat sides of wok and heat until oil just begins to smoke. Add garlic and ginger and a pinch of salt. Stir-fry until golden brown. Add shrimp and stir-fry until shrimp are pink and firm. Remove from wok and set aside. Wipe wok with a paper towel. To wok add 1 table-spoon peanut oil and swirl oil to coat sides. Heat until oil just begins to smoke. Add spinach, stir-fry for 15 seconds, and add soy sauce and rice sticks. Stir-fry 2 to 3 minutes, until rice sticks are heated through. Return shrimp to wok and add chicken broth. Stir-fry for 1 to 2 minutes. Add more soy sauce to taste and stir-fry to combine. Remove to a serving dish and garnish with green onion and a few drops Chinese hot oil. Serve at once.

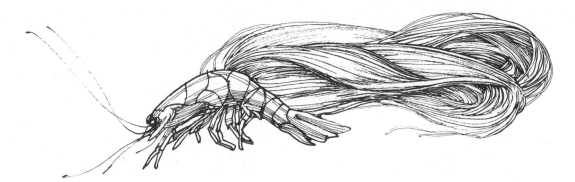

Have Velvet Chicken and noodles prepared ahead of time and then you can quickly assemble this appetizing dish. Serve it with a crisp salad and you have a meal in a hurry.

Stir-Fry Velvet Chicken with Noodles and Vegetables *Serves 4*

1 pound fine egg noodles
2 cups cooked Velvet Chicken (see page 78), shredded
2 cloves garlic, smashed and minced
2 slices ginger root, smashed and minced
2 cups bean sprouts, washed and drained thoroughly
1 green bell pepper, shredded
7 fresh mushrooms, sliced
3 soaked dried black mushrooms (see page 28), sliced
1 green onion, shredded
Peanut oil
2 tablespoons light soy sauce
2 tablespoons oyster sauce
½ cup chicken broth or liquid reserved from soaking mushrooms
Salt
Water

PREPARATION: Cook noodles according to package directions, drain well and set aside. Place velvet chicken, prepared garlic, ginger, bean sprouts, green pepper, fresh and soaked mushrooms and green onion on a large platter. Set aside. In a small bowl, combine 1/4 cup oil, soy sauce, oyster sauce and broth. Set aside. Have salt, water and oil ready to add as needed.

METHOD: Heat wok and add 1 tablespoon oil. With spatula, swirl oil around sides of wok and heat until oil just begins to smoke. Add garlic and ginger and stir-fry until golden brown. Add green pepper and stir-fry for 1 minute. Add fresh mushrooms, stir-fry briefly, add black mushrooms and bean sprouts. Add 1/2 teaspoon salt and sprinkle 1 tablespoon water down sides of wok. Stir-fry until vegetables are tender crisp. Remove from wok and set aside. To wok add 3 tablespoons oil and heat until oil just begins to smoke. Add noodles and stir-fry for 4 to 5 minutes, until noodles are heated through. Add chicken, stir-fry to combine and return vegetables to wok. Stir-fry to combine. Add soy sauce mixture and stir-fry to blend thoroughly. Remove to serving plate, garnish with green onion and serve at once.

Noodles, called mein, are used in combination with meats, vegetables and seafood. When beef is stir-fried and served over soft noodles it becomes a marvelous one-dish dinner.

Stir-Fry Beef Lo Mein *Serves 2*

½ pound beef flank steak, sliced
4 teaspoons cornstarch
2 tablespoons light soy sauce
1 teaspoon Chinese rice wine or
    dry sherry
4 quarts water
    Salt
8 ounces fine egg noodles,
2 cloves garlic, smashed and minced
2 slices ginger root, smashed and
    minced
1 cup green peas *or* 1 cup celery,
    sliced diagonally
2 green onions, minced
1 cup chicken broth
1 tablespoon oyster sauce
    Peanut oil
    Sesame oil

PREPARATION: In a small bowl, combine sliced flank steak, 2 teaspoons cornstarch, 1 tablespoon soy sauce and wine. Set aside for 15 to 20 minutes. In a large saucepan, bring 2 quarts water with 1/8 teaspoon salt to a boil. Add egg noodles and simmer until *just barely* cooked. Drain at once and rinse immediately in cold water. Set aside. In saucepan, bring 2 quarts water to boiling, cover and allow to simmer until needed. Prepare garlic, ginger, green peas and green onions. Set aside. In a small bowl, combine broth, 2 teaspoons cornstarch, 1 tablespoon soy sauce and oyster sauce. Set aside. Have peanut oil and sesame oil at hand.

METHOD: Heat wok and add 1 tablespoon peanut oil. With spatula, swirl oil around to coat sides of wok and heat until oil begins to smoke. Add peas and stir-fry until tender crisp, about 2 minutes. Remove from wok and set aside. To wok add 2 tablespoons peanut oil and, with spatula, swirl oil to coat sides of wok. Heat until oil just begins to smoke. Add garlic and ginger and stir-fry until golden brown. Add beef, spreading it in a single layer, and stir-fry 1 to 2 minutes. Make a well and add broth mixture; stir-fry until sauce thickens, about 2 to 3 minutes. Return peas to wok; add green onions and 4 to 5 drops sesame oil. Stir-fry to combine and add salt to taste. Immerse noodles in boiling water for 1 minute, drain thoroughly and place in serving dish. Top with steak mixture and serve at once.

Steamed Meat Dumplings *Makes 60 to 80 dumplings*

1	pound lean ground pork butt
10	water chestnuts, minced
1	slice ginger root, smashed and minced
4	soaked dried black mushrooms (see page 28), minced
1	green onion, minced
¼	cup fresh cilantro, minced
2	tablespoons cornstarch
¼	cup chicken broth or water
1	tablespoon light soy sauce
1	tablespoon sugar
2	teaspoons Chinese rice wine or dry sherry
80	homemade or 1 (1 lb.) package ready-made won ton wrappers
	Green peas or shredded carrots (optional)
	Dipping sauce: sesame oil mixed with soy sauce *or* Chinese hot oil mixed with soy sauce

PREPARATION: In a bowl, thoroughly combine pork, minced water chestnuts, ginger, mushrooms, green onion, cilantro, cornstarch, broth, soy sauce, sugar and wine. Set aside. Cut the corners off won ton wrappers, making each one round. (Keep won ton wrappers covered as much as possible with a damp towel or plastic wrap to prevent drying.) Have peas at hand and dipping sauce prepared.

METHOD: Place 1 rounded teaspoon pork filling in the center of each wrapper. Gather the edges up around the filling to make a small cup. Squeeze gently. Press bottom flat so dumpling will stand upright. Garnish each dumpling with a single pea or shredded carrots, if desired. Heat 2 to 3 cups water to boiling in wok or other pan equipped for steaming. Place dumplings in an oiled heatproof dish, on oiled steam plate or in bamboo steamer. Steam for 15 to 20 minutes. Serve at once with dipping sauce.

Pot Stickers *Makes approximately 50 pot stickers*

50   pot sticker wrappers, homemade
        or ready-made
Filling:
    1 cup finely chopped celery
        cabbage
    1 teaspoon salt
    1 pound lean ground pork butt
    1 egg, lightly beaten
    1 slice ginger root, smashed and
        minced
    3 tablespoons light soy sauce
    2 green onions, minced
    4 drops sesame oil
    1 teaspoon cornstarch
    1 tablespoon dry sherry
    1 tablespoon water
Beaten egg white or water
Peanut oil
Chicken or beef broth

To make pot sticker filling: Sprinkle celery cabbage with salt and let stand for 5 to 8 minutes. Drain and squeeze free of moisture. In a bowl, combine celery cabbage, ground pork, beaten egg, ginger, light soy sauce, green onions, sesame oil, cornstarch, sherry and water. Mix well to combine thoroughly and let rest for 20 to 30 minutes. If you wish, mixture may be made ahead to this point and stored for a day or two tightly covered in the refrigerator.

To fill pot stickers: Holding a pot sticker wrapper in your hand, place 1 rounded tablespoon filling in the center. Moisten the nearest edge with egg white. Make 4 to 6 tiny pleats along the nearest edge by pushing dough to the left with your thumb. Pinch to seal pleats. Fold wrapper over to close and pinch to seal tightly. Repeat until all filling has been used. If you have difficulty making pleats, you can just press the edges together flat; the flavor will not be affected. (Keep pot sticker wrappers covered with a damp towel or plastic wrap as much as possible to prevent drying.)

To cook pot stickers: Heat a large frying pan which has a tight-fitting lid and pour in just enough oil to cover the bottom with a light film. Heat until oil just begins to smoke and carefully place pot stickers in pan, allowing space between each. Brown pot stickers well on one side only. Add 1/2 cup chicken or beef broth, cover immediately and allow pot stickers to steam for 15 minutes. After 10 minutes, check to see if broth has almost evaporated. If not, remove cover for last 5 minutes of cooking.

To serve pot stickers: Place pot stickers brown side up on a serving plate. Let each guest make his or her own dipping sauce from one or more of the following condiments: light or dark soy sauce, Chinese hot oil, rice wine vinegar, sesame oil and chopped cilantro.

To store pot stickers: Uncooked filled pot stickers may be frozen up to 6 weeks. To freeze, arrange pot stickers 1 inch apart on a baking sheet and place in the freezer. When pot stickers are frozen, remove from baking sheet, wrap well and return to freezer.

Pot Sticker Wrappers *Makes 50 to 60 wrappers*

2½   cups all-purpose flour
1   cup hot tap water
    Cornstarch

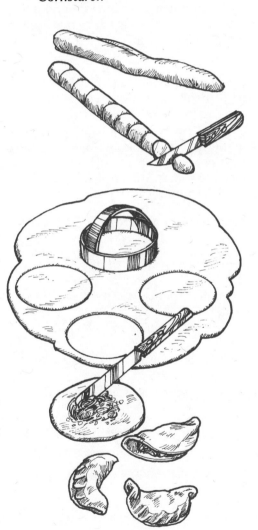

In a large bowl, measure all-purpose flour and gradually add hot tap water, mixing with a fork to blend thoroughly. When mixture becomes very heavy, remove dough from bowl and continue to blend with your hands on bread board. Knead dough well, about 5 minutes. Cover with a damp towel or plastic wrap and let rest for 20 minutes.

Shape dough in any of these three ways. Remember this dough dries very quickly. While shaping it, keep the dough covered as much as possible with a damp towel or plastic wrap.

To shape dough traditionally: Cut dough into quarters and roll each quarter into a rope 12 inches long and 1 inch thick. Cut ropes in 1 inch pieces; roll each piece with a rolling pin into a 3½ inch round.

To shape dough with a noodle machine: Divide dough into 6 pieces. With the noodle machine at the widest setting, pass dough through once or twice. Reset machine to next setting and roll dough, continuing to decrease the thickness of the setting until dough is as thin as a quarter. Cut dough into 3½ inch rounds with a cookie cutter.

To shape dough easily by hand: Roll dough out with a rolling pin until it is as thin as a quarter. Cut dough into 3½ inch rounds with a cookie cutter.

Dust wrappers with cornstarch and wrap tightly in plastic wrap. Wrappers will keep in the refrigerator for 3 to 4 days or in the freezer indefinitely. (Be sure to defrost frozen wrappers thoroughly before filling.)

One of the most delicious mysteries on restaurant menus can be made at home with amazing ease. You'll enjoy the marvelous freshness of homemade Won Ton in soups, as appetizers or even as entrées.

Shrimp and Pork Filled Won Ton *Makes approximately 80 won ton*

80 homemade or 1 (1 lb.) package
    ready-made won ton wrappers
Filling:
    ½ pound lean ground pork butt
    ½ pound shrimp, shelled, deveined,
       washed and dried
    2 tablespoons cornstarch
    1 tablespoon light soy sauce
    1 tablespoon Chinese rice wine
       or dry sherry
    2 green onions
    4 drops sesame oil
    1 egg, lightly beaten
    1 teaspoon salt
    Optional ingredients (see recipe)
Beaten egg white or water

If mixing filling by hand, thoroughly combine ground pork, minced shrimp, cornstarch, soy sauce, wine, minced green onions, sesame oil, egg, salt and any optional additions. Let mixture rest for 15 to 20 minutes.

If making filling in a food processor, cut green onions into 1 inch lengths. With steel blade in place, put green onions and any optional ingredients into work bowl. Quickly turn processor on and off 2 or 3 times. Add whole shrimp and quickly turn processor on and off 3 times. Add remaining ingredients. Quickly turn processor on and off 3 to 4 times. Do not over-process; mixture should still be slightly chunky. Let mixture rest for 15 to 20 minutes.

You may add one or more of the following ingredients to the won ton filling:

4 to 5 water chestnuts, minced *or* if to be processed,
   quartered
4 to 5 soaked dried black mushrooms (see page 28), minced
   or if to be processed, whole
1/2 to 1 cup celery cabbage, shredded *or*, if to be processed,
   cut into 2 inch pieces
2 tablespoons fresh coriander *or* cilantro, minced *or* if to
   be processed, whole
1 cup spinach, shredded *or* if to be processed, cut into
   2 inch pieces

Note: if using 2 or more optional ingredients, use 2 eggs instead of 1.

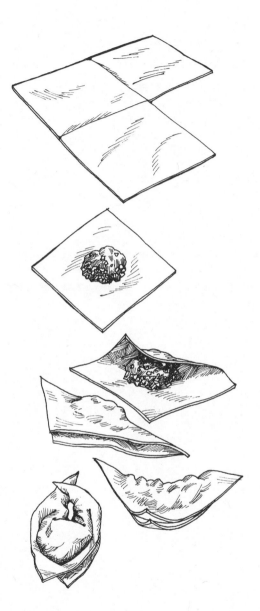

To fill won ton: In a large work space, have 1 or 2 damp towels and a baking sheet handy. Place one towel, folded in half, on baking sheet; as won ton are filled, place them on one half of the towel and cover with the other half. Always keep unfilled won ton skins covered with second damp towel or plastic wrap to prevent drying. On one won ton wrapper with one corner toward you, place 1/2 teaspoon filling in center of wrapper and moisten farthest corner with water. Fold wrapper in half to make a triangle and press to seal tightly. Moisten all points with water. Fold center point down even with lower edge. Hold won ton in both hands and fold back side points away from you. Overlap the edges and press firmly to seal. Place on damp towel and cover. Repeat until all are formed.

To boil won ton: This unusual method of boiling won ton removes the starch from won ton wrappers, keeps won ton from sticking together and retains the flavor of the filling.

In a 4 to 5 quart pot, bring 2 quarts water with 1 teaspoon salt to a boil. Gradually and carefully, so as not to radically change the temperature, add enough won ton to cover the bottom of the pot. Do not crowd. When water comes to a boil, add 1 to 1-1/2 cups cold water. Let water come to a second boil and add an additional 1 to 1-1/2 cups cold water. When water comes to a third boil, allow to boil for 2 minutes. Carefully remove won ton with a slotted spoon and drain on wire rack over paper towels. Repeat procedure, using the same water, to cook remaining won ton.

(If won ton are to be prepared at once in soup, you may omit the last two minutes of cooking. Remove won ton from pot after the second boil, add to hot broth and simmer 4 to 5 minutes, or as indicated in the recipe.)

Steamed won ton can be used in soups or served as part of a meal or as an appetizer with a dipping sauce.

In wok or other pan equipped for steaming, bring 2 to 3 cups water to a vigorous boil. Arrange won ton in a lightly oiled heatproof dish, on an oiled steam plate or in a bamboo steamer so that won ton do not touch. Lightly brush won ton with vegetable oil and steam for 10 to 15 minutes.

Steamed won ton may be made ahead and refrigerated for 1 or 2 days; if using in soup, be sure to bring won ton to room temperature before adding to broth.

Deep-fried won ton make a wonderful appetizer with a dipping sauce. Or, try them as part of a meal with Sweet and Sour Sauce (see page 65) poured over them. And, while usually only steamed or boiled won ton are used, many people enjoy the different texture and flavor of deep-fried won ton in soup.

In wok or other deep-frying pan, heat 3 cups peanut oil to 375° or until a cube of bread dropped in oil rises to surface and browns quickly. Add filled won ton, 6 or 7 at a time, and brown on one side, about 30 to 60 seconds. Turn to brown second side, about 15 to 30 seconds. Remove from oil and drain on tempura rack or paper towel. Repeat with remaining won ton. Kept in a plastic bag, deep-fried won ton will freeze well up to 4 weeks. To reheat, do not defrost; place on baking sheet and heat at 350° for 15 minutes or until hot.

Won Ton Wrappers or Egg Roll Wrappers *Makes 40 won ton wrappers, 10 egg roll wrappers*

2 cups bleached all-purpose flour
2 eggs
1½ tablespoons water (approximately)
    Cornstarch

In a mixing bowl, combine flour with eggs. Add water, enough to make a stiff dough, stirring to mix. On a lightly floured bread board, knead dough until very smooth, about 5 to 7 minutes. Cover with a damp towel or plastic wrap and let rest for 15 to 20 minutes. (This dough dries very quickly. Keep it covered as much as possible with a damp towel or plastic wrap.) Recipe may be doubled.

To roll out dough by hand, divide dough in half, and, with a lightly floured rolling pin, roll out one half dough into a rectangle until it is as thin as a dime.

If using a noodle machine to roll out dough, divide dough in thirds and, with machine at its widest setting, roll one third dough through machine once or twice. Adjust to a thinner setting and repeat. If dough becomes unmanageable, cut it in half and proceed. Repeat this procedure, adjusting to thinner settings until dough is as thin as a dime.

To make won ton wrappers: With a very sharp knife, cut dough into 3-1/2 inch squares and dust well with cornstarch. Stack squares and wrap tightly in plastic wrap. Repeat with remaining dough.

To make egg roll wrappers: Follow directions for won ton wrappers, rolling out dough until it is as thin as a dime. With a sharp knife, cut dough into 7 inch squares. Dust with cornstarch and wrap tightly in plastic wrap.

Any leftover dough may be cut into noodles. These can be cooked in water or broth for 2 minutes and enjoyed as pasta.

Egg Rolls   *Makes 16 egg rolls*

16   Egg Roll Wrappers, see page 117,
      or 1 (1 lb.) package ready-
      made wrappers
Filling:
      ¾ pound ham or Chinese barbe-
         cued pork, shredded (about
         2 cups)
      ½ pound bean sprouts, washed
         and thoroughly drained
      5 water chestnuts, shredded
      ½ cup shredded bamboo shoots
      2 ribs celery, sliced diagonally
         and shredded
      2 green onions, shredded
      1 (4 oz.) can mushrooms, well
         drained and shredded, liquid
         reserved
      1 tablespoon light soy sauce
      1 tablespoon oyster sauce
      ½ teaspoon sugar
      1 tablespoon Chinese rice wine
         or dry sherry
      2 tablespoons cornstarch
      ¼ cup liquid reserved from
         canned mushrooms
Fresh cilantro (optional)
Beaten egg
Peanut oil, for deep-frying

To make filling: On a platter, arrange prepared ham, bean sprouts, water chestnuts, bamboo shoots, celery, green onions and mushrooms. Set aside. In a small bowl, combine soy sauce, oyster sauce, sugar, wine, cornstarch and liquid from canned mushrooms. Set aside. Have peanut oil at hand. Heat wok and add 2 tablespoons oil. With a spatula, swirl oil around sides of wok and heat until oil just begins to smoke. Add bean sprouts and stir-fry 1 minute. Add celery and stir-fry 1 minute. Add water chestnuts, bamboo shoots and mushrooms. Stir-fry to heat through. Make a well and add soy sauce mixture. Stir-fry to combine. Add ham and green onion, stir-frying carefully; mixture will be thick. Remove from wok, place in colander to drain and let cool.

To fill the egg rolls: In a large work area, place egg roll wrapper with one point toward you. Place 3 to 4 table-spoons filling and a small sprig of cilantro on lowest third of wrapper. Rolling away from you, roll nearest point to just enclose filling. Moisten all edges with egg. Fold in side points and press to seal. Roll to wrap filling completely and press to seal edges. Repeat until all wrappers are filled. (Keep egg roll wrappers covered with a damp towel or plastic wrap as much as possible to prevent drying out.)

To fry egg rolls: In wok or other deep-frying pan, heat 3 to 4 cups peanut oil to 375° or until a cube of bread dropped in oil rises to the surface and browns quickly. With bamboo tongs, carefully put 4 or 5 egg rolls in oil, one at a time. Brown on all sides, about 3 to 4 minutes. Remove and drain on tempura rack or paper towels. Serve hot with Chinese hot mustard or a dipping sauce made of Chinese hot oil and soy sauce.

Egg rolls may be deep-fried ahead and reheated in 350° oven for 7 to 10 minutes. Or, keep deep-fried egg rolls frozen until ready to use. To reheat, do not defrost. Just heat frozen egg rolls in 350° oven for 15 to 20 minutes or until hot.

Mandarin Pancakes *Makes 16 pancakes*

1 cup boiling water
2 cups all-purpose flour
   Vegetable oil

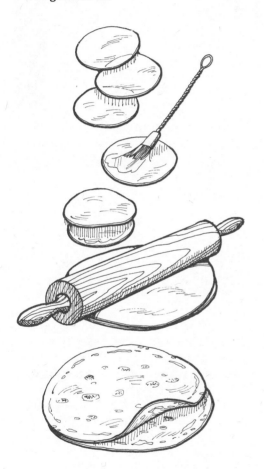

In a bowl, gradually add boiling water to flour, mixing well until thoroughly combined. On a lightly floured board, knead dough until smooth, about 5 to 10 minutes. Cover with a damp towel or plastic wrap and let rest 20 minutes. Divide dough in half, roll each half into a log 8 inches long and 1 inch in diameter. Cut into 1 inch pieces and press each piece into a 2 to 3 inch round. Brush the top of 2 rounds with oil and place one on top of the other, oiled sides together. With a rolling pin, evenly roll out double round into a 7 inch circle. Set aside and cover with a damp towel or plastic wrap. Repeat until all rounds have been rolled.

To cook, heat a griddle or large frying pan until water dances when sprinkled on the surface. Brush griddle with oil and cook pancakes, 1 or 2 at a time, heating on 1 side until a light brown specks appear, about 30 to 60 seconds. Turn and bake other side, about 15 to 30 seconds. Remove pancakes from heat and pull two pieces apart. Cover with aluminum foil and keep warm. Repeat until all pancakes are cooked. Fold cooked pancakes into triangles, place on a serving plate and serve at once.

Pancakes may be made ahead, wrapped in foil and refrigerated for up to 5 days. Or freeze pancakes, wrapped in aluminum foil, for up to 3 months. To reheat, heat thawed pancakes in foil in a 350° oven for 10 to 15 minutes or until warm and pliable.

Light Desserts

Traditionally, the Chinese do not serve desserts with their family meals. Sweets are eaten, however, as snacks and at formal banquets. If you wish, you may finish your Chinese dinner with some fresh fruit—or one of these light and tempting favorites.

Sesame Seed Cookies *Makes 28 cookies*

When eating in a Chinese restaurant you are usually served a few cookies at the end of the meal. Sesame cookies are often among the selection. You'll find they are so easy to make at home and much more delicious than their restaurant counterparts. Chances are you'll make them every time you want a quick batch of cookies for lunch or dinner.

1¼	cups all-purpose flour, unsifted
¾	teaspoon baking powder
½	teaspoon five spice powder (optional)
½	teaspoon salt
½	cup brown sugar, firmly packed
½	cup corn oil
1	egg
1	teaspoon vanilla
¼	cup toasted sesame seeds (see below)

In a large bowl, combine flour, baking powder, five spice powder, salt, brown sugar, corn oil, egg and vanilla. Combine thoroughly. Have toasted sesame seeds at hand on wax paper. Form dough into a log 1-1/2 inches in diameter and 14 inches long. With a sharp knife, cut log in half lengthwise to form two logs. Cut each log into 1 inch pieces. Roll each piece into ball and gently dip in sesame seeds. Place on an ungreased baking sheet, sesame seed side up, about 1 inch apart. Flatten cookies with a fork and bake at 350° for 8 to 10 minutes, or until cookies are lightly browned around the edges. Cool on wire rack. Cookies will stay fresh stored in an airtight container for 2 to 3 days.

To toast sesame seeds, place seeds in a frying pan over medium heat and cook, stirring occasionally, until golden brown. Remove to wax paper and set aside.

If you happen to have a few won ton wrappers on hand, you have some delightful cookies only minutes away. Bow Cookies are a marvelous example of Chinese thrift. Rather than throw leftover wrappers away, they deep-fry them for sweet treats during the day.

Bow Cookies *Makes 48 cookies*

24 won ton wrappers
2 cups peanut oil for deep-frying
¼ cup powdered sugar
½ teaspoon cinnamon (optional)

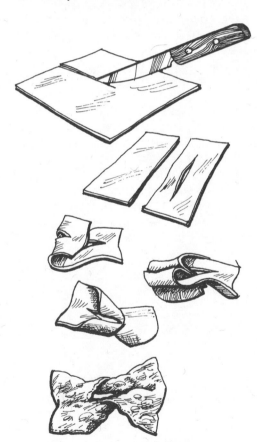

PREPARATION: Cut won ton wrappers in half to make each piece 1-3/4 by 3-1/2 inches. Make a 3/4 inch slit lengthwise down the center of each piece and pull one end of the wrapper through the slit to make a bow. Repeat until all wrappers are used. Combine powdered sugar and cinnamon in shaker.

METHOD: In a wok or other deep-frying pan, heat oil to 375° or until a cube of bread dropped in oil rises to the surface and browns quickly. Add bows, 4 to 5 at a time and turn immediately with bamboo tongs. Allow one side to brown, about 15 to 20 seconds, and turn to brown other side, about 5 to 10 seconds. Remove bows from wok and drain on tempura rack or paper towel. Repeat until all bows are done. Remove cookies to a dry paper towel and sprinkle with powdered sugar. Cookies will stay fresh 3 to 4 days in a tightly sealed container.

Here is the sweet version of filled won ton. The Chinese often make these cookies with candied winter melon but the cookies are equally as good filled with candied cherries or other such fruit. They are so easy to make and the whole family will enjoy them for after-dinner snacks.

Crescent Cookies *Makes 48 to 60 cookies*

½ cup coconut flakes
½ cup salted cocktail peanuts, coarsely chopped
½ cup candied cherries or other type of candied fruit, chopped
½ cup brown sugar, firmly packed
½ cup white sugar
1 egg or egg white, lightly beaten
  Won ton wrappers, round type if available, about 48 to 60
3 cups peanut oil for deep-frying

PREPARATION: In a bowl, combine coconut flakes, peanuts, cherries, brown sugar and white sugar. Set aside. In a small bowl, beat egg lightly and set aside. If using square won ton wrappers, fold each into a triangle and cut off the top corner. In the center of each won ton wrapper, place 2 teaspoons filling. Moisten edges with beaten egg and fold diagonally into a crescent. Press to seal edges tightly all around so that filling will not escape while cooking. Set aside. Continue until filling is gone. Have tempura rack or paper towel handy.

METHOD: In a wok or other deep-frying pan, heat oil to 350° or until a cube of bread dropped in oil rises to the surface and browns quickly. (Do not allow oil to overheat or cookies will burn.) With bamboo tongs or a slotted spoon, carefully put 6 or 7 cookies into oil. Turn each cookie almost immediately, as soon as the edges turn white. Brown on one side, about 20 to 30 seconds; turn and brown the other side, about 10 seconds. Drain on tempura rack or paper towel. Repeat until all cookies are done.

Cookies will remain fresh for 3 to 4 days if stored in an airtight container.

Almond Cookies are another popular dessert in restaurants. Here is a recipe using the refrigerator method. Simply make the dough, refrigerate it and bake the cookies at your convenience.

Refrigerator Almond Cookies   *Makes 48 cookies*

1¼   cups all-purpose flour
½   teaspoon baking powder
¼   teaspoon salt
½   cup lard or other solid
      shortening
½   cup sugar
2   eggs
1½   teaspoons almond extract
48   whole blanched almonds
1   teaspoon water

In a small bowl, combine flour, baking powder and salt. Set aside. In a large bowl, cream shortening and sugar. Add 1 egg and almond extract. Stir to combine. Add flour mixture and blend thoroughly, until dough is smooth and soft. Divide dough in half and place each half on a sheet of waxed paper. Form each half into a log 1-1/2 inches thick and about 12 inches long. Wrap logs in waxed paper and refrigerate for several hours or overnight. When firm, slice logs into pieces 1/4 inch thick. Place slices 1 inch apart on a greased baking sheet. Press a whole almond into the center of each cookie. In a small bowl, combine 1 egg with 1 teaspoon water. Brush each cookie with egg glaze and bake in a 375° oven for 10 to 12 minutes, or until cookies are lightly browned. Remove cookies from oven and cool on wire rack. Cookies will stay fresh 3 to 4 days in a tightly sealed container.

Ginger Ice Cream   *Makes 1 quart*

One of the simplest and most refreshing Chinese desserts can be made with preserved ginger and a good quality vanilla ice cream. Preserved ginger (ginger cooked in a heavy sugar syrup) is available in earthenware jars in oriental markets.

Soften 1 quart of vanilla ice cream. Mince enough preserved ginger to make 6 tablespoons. Fold minced ginger along with 6 tablespoons ginger syrup into softened ice cream. Refreeze for 4 to 5 hours. Garnish individual servings with toasted sesame seeds or almonds.

To make last minute ginger sundaes: Mince 1 tablespoon preserved ginger per serving and spoon ginger with 1 tablespoon syrup over individual servings of ice cream. Garnish with toasted sesame seeds or almonds.

Every lover of Chinese food is familiar with the classic Almond Float. Originated in Peking, the authentic Almond Float is made with agar-agar (a gelatinous seaweed derivative) and ground blanched almonds. However, it is easily made with gelatin, evaporated milk and almond extract. I could not resist also adding beaten egg white and crushed pineapple for a new, lighter Almond Float. My interpretation, like the original, is also served in syrup and accented with chilled fruit.

Fluffy Almond Float *Serves 4*

1	envelope unflavored gelatin
3	tablespoons cold water
½	cup evaporated milk
1¼	cups water
6	tablespoons sugar
3	teaspoons almond extract
1	egg white
1	can crushed pineapple, well drained and liquid reserved
	Syrup (see recipe)
	Fruit, well drained and chilled

In a small, heavy saucepan, stir gelatin into 3 tablespoons cold water. Stir over low heat until gelatin dissolves. Add milk, 1-1/4 cups water and 4 tablespoons sugar. Continue to stir until sugar is completely dissolved. Remove from heat and add 2 teaspoons almond extract. Mixture will be lukewarm. Pour into a bowl and refrigerate for 1 to 2 hours, or until mixture is almost set. Remove from refrigerator and beat at medium speed with an electric mixer for 30 seconds. Set aside. In a large bowl, beat egg white until light. Add 2 tablespoons sugar and 1 teaspoon almond extract and continue to beat until soft peaks form. With a rubber spatula, fold in gelatin mixture and 1/2 cup drained, crushed pineapple. Mound into individual serving dishes and refrigerate until ready to serve. (If made more than 4 hours prior to serving, cover loosely with plastic wrap.) Just before serving, garnish each serving with remaining crushed pineapple, syrup and any of the following drained, chilled fruit: lychees, loquats, mandarin oranges, apricots or maraschino cherries.

To make syrup: Combine reserved pineapple juice plus enough water to make 1 cup liquid and 1/4 cup sugar in a heavy saucepan. Stir over low heat until sugar completely dissolves. Mixture will be thin and lukewarm. Remove from heat and set aside to cool.

Index